MODERN STEAM ROAD WAGONS 1906

MODERN STEAM ROAD WAGONS 1906

by

WILLIAM NORRIS

David & Charles Reprints

ISBN 0 7153 5909 6

First published by Longmans, Green and Co., in 1906
This photo-litho reprint published in 1972

Printed in Great Britain by
Redwood Press Limited, Trowbridge, Wiltshire
for David & Charles (Publishers) Limited
Newton Abbot Devon

PREFACE

CARE has been taken to include in this book particulars of the latest, and—by reason of the 1905 Board of Trade Regulations—important modifications and designs of heavy steam road wagons; and to give an accurate and impartial analytical account of past and present practice.

With this object, illustrations and drawings necessary to explain the text are extensively made use of; and it is hoped that the publication may serve a purpose alike useful to manufacturers and users—present or prospective—as an intelligent aid to manufacturers to design and as a medium for users to enable them to select the best possible vehicles to fit their particular requirements. Particular attention has been devoted to constructional details to show what has been attempted in the past, the shortcomings which experience manifested, and how and what improvements have, from time to time, been made to overcome, one by one, the difficulties and deficiencies as they arose.

The majority of the outline technical drawings have been made under the author's own supervision and are new, and it is to be hoped will be found serviceable to the end he has in view.

This is the first publication which has in any way attempted to deal exclusively with the subject of heavy steam motor wagons. It is difficult at such a relatively early stage in the industry to collect what is, generally, fragmentary and widely

diffused data ; and my thanks are tendered to the various manufacturers and users included. Willing response has been accorded
me from the majority.

The principles underlying steam for road haulage are better
appreciated and understood than any other power. Traction-
engine performances have, of course, been of enormous assistance
in the development of the lighter, faster, and modern road
wagons, and the types now existing have, in their essential
features, been little departed from in the past few years. Standard
and well-proved lines are becoming more evident. So much,
indeed, has the modern heavy steam road wagon proved successful and reliable that it is anticipated that the products of the
more prominent constructors will not for a considerable time—
with perhaps immaterial modifications—be departed from. By
this it is not implied that finality has been reached or even
approximated, but rather that present-day vehicles have attained
a thoroughly commercial standard, all essential qualifications to
render them so having now been well demonstrated and time-
proved.

Prospective users can be furnished with undeniable evidence
of the high degree of reliability reached and of the exact cost
of operating heavy steam wagons in comparison with older
methods of haulage, to the general advantage of the newer means.
For some purposes—very short journeys necessitating numerous
calls and stoppages—mechanical wagons have not yet shown a
sufficient saving over the horse to warrant their substitution, but
for other than this restricted sphere pronounced economy can
be shown.

That such reliable and economic results have been obtained
in so short a time—the problem of superseding horse haulage by
mechanical power being one of the most difficult yet presented
to the engineer—is a highly meritorious achievement, the more
striking inasmuch as, in many instances, the pioneers were not

previously engaged in allied work, and were until 1896, owing to prohibitive laws, given no incentive to creative efforts in this direction.

The manufacture of transport vehicles is now engaging the attention of a large number of engineering firms, evidence being abundant to show that the industry is fast assuming big proportions. How far steam as the motive power may be employed cannot well be truly predicted, but for the heavier classes of vehicles there is no doubt it will hold its own against any known power for a long time.

It is patent in several new models of heavy steam wagons, however, that, on account of the absence of reliable data, old ideas are apt to be reintroduced—ideas which have been proved by the pioneer firms who have been "through the mill" to be untenable or unsuitable in application to heavy road wagons; and if the author, in pointing out some of the pitfalls of the past, serves to guard against their future reintroduction, another of his objects will be performed.

For valuable assistance rendered him by Mr. Allan Fergusson on the drawings and Mr. W. Nelson Bower for his assistance in the preparation of the chapter on Lubrication, the author desires to record his best thanks.

W. NORRIS.

CONTENTS

LIST OF ILLUSTRATIONS

xiv LIST OF ILLUSTRATIONS

MODERN
STEAM ROAD WAGONS

INTRODUCTION

THE object of this treatise is not to deal with the subject of heavy steam road vehicles from the scientific standpoint, nor to enter into tabulations understood only by those devoted to refinements in calculation, but rather to deal broadly with the question of generating and using steam in its successful application for propulsion of these particular vehicles.

The historical aspect of the question is exceedingly interesting and should not be lost sight of, but is ably dealt with in many previous publications. The Liverpool trials (see Appendix) show the practical outcome of the efforts of the pioneers of the modern heavy road vehicle; and the summaries thereto attached, in which the results have been embodied in tabulated form, warrant careful study. A good amount of progress has been made since the termination of those trials in 1901; but the dream of the pioneers who spent large sums of money, starting practically *de novo* without the aid of the knowledge which is now available and with the law of the land against them, has perhaps scarcely been realized. We, however, owe much to these enthusiastic initiators, and that many of them are now reaping the fruit of their early efforts is but a fitting recompense. In a new industry, having experiments as its only basis, many mistakes are necessarily to be expected. We have only to look back at the first trials in 1889 in Liverpool, and compare the vehicles then competing with those in the Liverpool trials, 1901, to see how much had to be discarded or improved. These latter trials were eminently successful for the short period over which they extended; and many enthusiasts, seeing how well the vehicles ran throughout that short time, thought that finality was in view and production of standard vehicles in quantities realizable; but, unfortunately, time revealed faults, and the endeavour since has been to gradually eradicate those weaknesses as they manifested themselves in actual work, and important and steady—rather than radical—improvements have been effected, with the result that the present-day heavy steam road vehicle has long passed its experimental stage and thoroughly established its reputation as a commercial success.

In designing these vehicles, not only is it absolutely necessary that the strains should be properly distributed, combining the lightest possible construction with the greatest strength, but that simplicity—inasmuch as we are dealing with a commercial article —must be ever kept in view.

The two most difficult problems which have been encountered are, undoubtedly, to design a fitting boiler and proper road wheels.

It does not, by any means, follow that a boiler giving the utmost satisfaction when used for stationary purposes will be at all suitable for road vehicles. It is well known that the power of the boiler, or, more accurately, the amount of steam that it can furnish in a given time, depends, first of all, upon its area of heating surface; and the amount of steam that a square foot of heating surface will produce varies between very wide limits, affected, as it is, by a number of conditions. Of course, a boiler's function is to transfer as much as possible of the heat of combustion to the water, and the heating surface must be adapted to this end.

The amount of heat generated which can be transferred and the amount of heat actually transferred in a given time vary with the amount of the heating surface exposed. The capacity and economy of a boiler rests, therefore, upon not its declared heating surface, but upon its "effective" heating surface. For stationary purposes "forcing" is of very rare occurrence, but on most roads the "peak" must be met many times in the course of an hour. To illustrate more clearly, we will take the square or oblong (fire or water tubed) with a circular burner in the centre of the boiler. We here neglect, to a very large extent, the corner tubes, and considerably hamper the circulation. Now, if we take a circular water-tube boiler with a circular burner, which will envelop, say, three of its four rows of tubes, we then have a more uniform heating area, with the outer row of tubes acting as down-comers. In the case of a circular fire-tube boiler, the flame will envelop the furnace crown and then pass up the tubes some distance before losing that intensity of heat which renders it visible, the products of combustion passing into the chimney at a low temperature. Therefore the value of a square foot of heating surface depends mainly upon the relative portion and direction in which the current of heated products obtains contact with the metallic surfaces. Whilst a low temperature in the smoke stack is essential to economy of fuel, at the same time a high temperature is necessary to superheat the exhaust steam led into the chimney to render it invisible as required by law.

The difficulty in obtaining water and the varying qualities thereof make it next to impossible to use any scale preventative which will be effective against the diversity of impregnations encountered. Probably ordinary petroleum, fed by means of a sight-feed lubricator into the boiler, gives the best results.

Although the boiler has received much attention (and much study will yet have to be given to produce the best possible combinations for road vehicle use), road wheels have, somehow, been sadly neglected. Amongst the earliest types steel built-up wheels and ordinary lorry wheels were tried, but neither pattern gave satisfaction. Then the gun-carriage wheel was introduced with better success, and composite wheels, having steel centres and the usual felloes and tyres, are being used by some makers. Quite apart from what diameter of wheel and width of tyre is necessary for a given load, there is something more important to consider. In the "Engineer," 4 November, 1904, a very able leader appeared on road vehicles. The following is an abstract: "The engineer who wishes to make his machines popular will make them silent. The wheel which has the capability of absorbing road shocks at its place of contact with the ground will be comparatively silent, and upkeep will then be *reduced* to a large extent." The "Engineer" again, in an article on road wheels (20 January, 1905), says: "The problem presented to the inventor is much more difficult of solution than appears at first sight. The solution will never be reached unless it is fully recognized that the wheel and the road constitute a mechanical combination which must be dealt with as a whole."

All steam wagons appear to be now fitted with compound reversing engines. There is, however, a great difference of opinion as to size of cylinders, revolutions per minute, single or other eccentric reversing gear, block pistons, hollow versus balanced flat valves, etc.

At the first blush, compounding with a $3\frac{1}{2}$ in. high-pressure cylinder looks anything but the correct practice for loads of, say, four tons. The author has made a considerable number of experiments with two high-pressure cylinders fitted with Stephenson's link gear with various degrees of " cut off." The result of these experiments amply demonstrated that, under all conditions of working, there is a decided gain in favour of the compound engine; yet although the economy in compounding was thus, to him, firmly established, he is still of opinion that, for small powers, high-pressure engines might prove more favourable.

During the past fifteen years considerable progress has been made in high-speed engines, and reliable data are now available which prove beyond all doubt that this class of engine can be relied on—prophecies to the contrary notwithstanding—and that greater signs of wear in a given period are not more observable than in ordinary slow-running engines. The advantages of " high speed " are practically acknowledged by the majority of makers who run their engines as fast as they consider prudent, each one, however, disapproving very strongly of speeds above that to which he finds himself limited.

A modern high-speed engine makes 500 revolutions per minute, with a piston speed of 500 ft. per minute. Relatively, indeed, to those speeds which past practice tolerated, 500 revolutions per minute is very high ; but, considered absolutely, and as it appears to all persons accustomed to it, the speed of the modern high-speed engine is but natural, and, on all counts, the desirable speed at which a properly designed and constructed engine ought to be run for the special purposes of its employment—road wagons.

The tendency is to make the engine and gearing self-contained, with all the moving parts running in a bath of oil. This arrange-

ment is highly satisfactory, and no trouble need be experienced
from a lubricating point of view, the "make up" being very
small. By repeated use of the same lubricant, a uniform rise of
temperature and expansion results. In order to maintain accuracy of fit, the outer portion of bearings should also be allowed
to expand by being kept warm. This is provided for by enclosing
the working parts and preventing the access of cold atmosphere.
Enclosing also introduces other advantages, inasmuch as all parts
are protected from grit and dust which would otherwise play a
detrimental part. In double-acting engines the reversal of pressure gives opportunity for the entrance of oil alternately to the
two sides of the bearings, for there is not in high-speed engines
sufficient time to squeeze out all the interposed film of oil before
reversal again comes into operation, hence the metal of the shafts
and bearings practically do not come into contact. The wear
taking place is infinitesimal; and where the "flooding" system
has been adopted, heating of bearings has been rendered a comparatively rare occurrence.

It is well to bear in mind, when engaged on designing a road
wagon, into whose hands it is likely to be entrusted. Could we
rely upon them being systematically overhauled, run, and adjusted
by skilled mechanics, as are railway locomotives, then there would
be no limit to the refinements to be introduced. It is the author's
experience, however, that refinements in details in motor-wagon
construction (no reliability can be attached to securing really first-
class men as drivers) can be extended to limits overrunning the
practical advantages which would accrue by such refinements if
under skilled supervision. Much trouble has been occasioned by
allowing the driver opportunities of making his "adjustments."
If bearings are made with ample surfaces, and are provided with
a continuous supply of lubricant, adjustment is not necessary for
some years. With these facts in mind the author introduced
non-adjustable bearings on the "Leyland" wagons for crank,
second motion, and compensating shafts, and results have more
than justified the wisdom of this "retrogression" in obviating
tampering by unskilled drivers.

The question of direct versus chain drive is a vexed one—
some makers favouring one, some the other. Better results are
said by some to be obtained by chain drive who formerly used a

direct method; but the fact is that the essence of success rests not with either system *per se*, but rather in the provision made in the general design for allowance of compensation to the inequalities of the road.   If we view a chain against a direct drive, and without considering any other factors, as the former is flexible and the track is constantly changing, the chain should, logically, be the better method; but other factors operating in a composite machine may so alter circumstances as to give the verdict to the direct drive.   There is no question that for a simple means of transmitting power the modern chain is a satisfactory solution, and other things being equal, the advantages of a chain drive are felt, because the power is constantly varying, and as the road is by no means constant, the whole mechanism has to be mounted on a more or less yielding frame.   The flexibility of the chain therefore assists to overcome the difficulties thus encountered.   In a direct drive some provision must be made equal to the provision found in the flexibility of the chain.   That being provided for, the two systems stand equal.

Against chain drives it is a fact that traction-engine makers many years ago satisfied themselves that transmission of power by means of the chains then available was unsatisfactory and in many ways unsuitable; but vast improvements have been made in the construction of chains of late years, and it would not be fair to argue that because traction-engine makers discarded the chains available years ago, that traction engines driving with modern chains might not prove just as satisfactory, or even more satisfactory, than the methods now adopted.   Besides, motor wagons travel much faster than traction engines, and the road shocks are proportionally increased.

Hans Renold, the well-known authority on chains, says: " In olden times driving chains were looked upon as jointed steel bands with gaps for teeth to enter; and the wheels were but discs with projections called teeth.   This, of course, has all changed, and, unless the tooth form and the wheel diameter are carefully designed according to definite laws, no satisfactory results can be obtained from chain driving."

The majority of the manufacturers of the North of England, where the worst roads are encountered, have favoured chain driving.   There are considerations pro and con both systems, and the advantages of the one over the other are not of a pronounced character ; and we may expect to find both being continued to be used according to the favour of the designers.

In reviewing the work done by heavy motor-wagon builders the absolute disregard of recovering the exhaust stands out prominently. In this respect practice has been retrogressive since 1898. Clarkson seems to be the only maker who has adhered at all to any method of condensing the exhaust steam. Many cooling systems used on petrol automobiles have been wonderfully successful and, with modifications, could be adapted to recover what is now wasted in steam wagons. With an efficient condenser it is possible that the same source of supply of water could always be used in the boiler—a very important thing—and what would do more, perhaps, than anything else to eliminate the shortcomings and inordinate amount of repairs to boilers necessitated by the indiscriminate use of varying water supplies.

The public have had it ocularly demonstrated to them that commercial motor wagons have long passed out of the experimental stage, for we have vehicles that have now been in actual daily work extending over periods of many years, and which, without inordinate expense in upkeep, continue to give satisfactory results. There is ample evidence also that the highest grade and most satisfactory business vehicles are the outcome of British firms, who are well to the fore against other countries in the practical application of heavy steam motor vehicles for commercial purposes. Many attempts have been made by the leading continental automobile manufacturers to put heavy motor wagons on the market, and, as if to prove that success in light car construction does not necessarily imply success in heavy traction (the problems involved are far removed), of the whole number of such attempts—and they have been many—only four at the present time have met with any degree of success. In America, owing to like faulty construction, little headway has been made.

The names of some of the most famous engineering firms are associated with the British products, and their reputation is sufficient to stamp their manufactures as of excellent workmanship and design. The traction-engine manufacturers have curiously (with one exception) stood aloof ; but nearly all of them have now decided to launch into the steam-wagon market, and with the data and experience furnished by the pioneer steam-lorry builders, combined with their long experience in traction-engine practice, we may expect to find some excellent additional types in the near future. These latter firms, with irreproachable reputations for traction engines, were probably desirous of seeing others work out the crudeness attending any new departure before venturing upon the manufacture themselves. They may have felt that any mistakes in a new line of manufacture would reflect on their existing reputations, and preferred to wait until the general industry had arrived at such a stage as by adopting the best available practice such a contingency would be remote. This may be " safe " practice, but the lack of initiative and enterprise on the part of the traction-engine builders, who in the natural course of events should have been best fitted for the manufacture of heavy steam wagons, is passing strange.

A great impetus has lately been given to the conversion of the public to heavy motors, and now that the 1905 regulations have been issued the demand for all kinds of business vehicles will probably be enormous.

Municipal authorities were one of the first bodies to seriously take up heavy motor vehicles, and they are now employed for refuse collecting, road making, scavenging, cleansing, etc.

All traders handling heavy loads—brewers, millers, colliery owners, and provision merchants being to the fore—now recognize how thoroughly satisfactory motor wagons have become both as time and money savers, and that to up-to-date and progressive firms they are indispensable.

Railways and carrying agencies are now placing extensive orders, and the demand must constantly increase, so that the time is not far distant when the industry will rank among one of the largest branches of engineering.

There is a vast field for the employment of motor wagons for agricultural purposes as tractors and motive power for the different operations of agriculturists, but more especially in the adaptation of these vehicles to convey farm produce to market or direct to customers without reloadings, and as a more economical means than is possible under existing railway transport.

There is no apparent ambiguity about the wording of the 1905 regulations, and, taking them altogether, makers and users ought to be fairly satisfied, although it is evidenced that the alarmist views which have from time to time been put forward by "authorities" have been somewhat arbitrarily accepted. Until the Highways and Locomotive Acts themselves can be constitutionally amended, the regulations should, in operation, serve to permit of heavy vehicles proving that they are not "road-destroyers," but are rather conducive to keeping roads in better and firmer condition. The rights of the public are well protected, and additional tare weights are conceded to manufacturers and users which should serve as a stimulus to renewed activity in production. The length of time occupied in formulating these regulations caused a serious slump in the demand, prospective users being naturally chary in placing their orders until it was seen exactly how the cat was going to jump.

It will be seen from the full text of the regulations given in the Appendix that all vehicles of 2 tons unladen weight will be thereby governed. The weight of an unloaded vehicle is raised to 5 tons. This is a quite unnecessary provision, however, seeing that the total vehicle-and-load limit is fixed at 12 tons, and the axle-weight being restricted to 8 tons on the driving wheels, this limit of 12 tons curtails inventive enterprise on the lines of making coupled-wheel drivers.

If the idea were to limit to 8 tons on any one axle, provision might have been made that this weight was the basis of computation for driving wheels, which would then have permitted a full-load weight of 16 tons in the case of a four-wheeled vehicle with all driving wheels, whilst the effect of such a load, so distributed, would have been exactly the same as is provided in the 12 tons limit.

No limit is fixed for the weight on the trailer beyond the fact that, together with the lorry, it must not exceed $6\frac{1}{2}$ tons, allowing, with a 5 ton vehicle, only $1\frac{1}{2}$ tons as the weight of the trailer. This seems an unnecessary restriction. Certainly, with a lighter vehicle, the weight of the trailer may be increased proportionately, but this has limits, remembering the tractive weight essential to draw a given load. The total load and tare of car and trailer must not exceed 20 tons—$13\frac{1}{2}$ and $6\frac{1}{2}$ tons respectively—in the case of a two-axled trailer 24 tons, viz. $6\frac{1}{2}$ tons tare weight of both and

17½ tons distributed load. According to present experience, however, a 5 ton tare car or trailer is scarcely equal to a load of 13½ tons, so that the extra axle would be of no practical use. What constitutes "tare weight" of a vehicle is still left an open question, although the Local Government Board's circular implies that in certain cases a detachable body or framework might be considered part of the load rather than of the vehicle itself. Examples of such detachable bodies or framework might be corporation watering-cart tanks, delivery-van bodies, refrigerating chambers, and oil tanks for oil companies' supply wagons.

Car wheels must be of not less than 24 in. in diameter, and the tyres, if of steel or other non-elastic construction, 5 in. wide, and the trailer wheels must also be of not less than 24 in. diameter with minimum 3 in. tyres. Makers of the heavier classes of vehicles will not resent these dimensions, but for vehicles of 2 tons tare or approximating this limit the minimum width of tyre, 5 in., seems disproportionate to requirements. As, however, in the majority of cases such lighter machines will be shod with rubber tyres, the framers of the regulations might have had this in view with a desire that elastic tyres should be used instead of metal wherever practical.

All vehicles under 3 tons tare with ordinary tyres are restricted to 8 miles an hour speed, and to 5 miles per hour if exceeding 3 tons tare weight or 6 tons axle weight, or for any car with a trailer. To facilitate reckonings a tabulated statement of minimum widths of wheels is issued with the regulations. That this is not an unnecessary provision is evidenced by the fact that this statement occupies more space than the whole of the detailed regulations. The diameter of the wheels, the axle weight, and the unit of axle weights are the three determining factors in arriving at the minimum width of tyre required. For example, for a wheel 3 ft. 3 in. in diameter and axle weight of 6 tons, the width of tyre would be 7½ in.; and for the same weight on a 6 ft. wheel it would be 6 in. The unit of registered weight is taken on a 3 ft. diameter wheel, the unit of registered axle weight being 7½ cwt. with an addition of 1 cwt. for every 12 in. by which the diameter is increased beyond 3 ft., and in the same proportion for any increase which is greater or less than 6 in.

For cars for military purposes 6 tons is permitted as tare weight in place of 5 tons; and the car and trailer may weigh up to 8 tons against $6\frac{1}{2}$ tons for ordinary vehicles, and where tyres are shod or fitted with diagonal crossbars 5 cwt. may be taken with 3 ft. diameter wheel as the basis of calculation instead of $7\frac{1}{2}$ cwt.

The rights of owners of bridges are carefully defined, and the clause should put an end to many annoyances owners have in the past been subjected to. Where conspicuous notices are erected that bridges are unsafe for heavy cars the registered axle weight of any axle of which exceeds 3 tons, or any greater weight specified in the notices, owners may stop all cars not complying therewith. If it is proved, after reference to arbitration, that a bridge is safe for the prohibited weights the prohibition shall be removed, but in place thereof another maximum weight may be substituted. Notice may be served upon bridge owners to refer to arbitration, and if concurrence thereto or neglect by the owner to appoint an arbitrator extends over one month, then all prohibitions notified shall be void.

No car having any one axle weight exceeding 6 tons shall be allowed to cross a bridge upon which there is another heavy car or traction engine.

No trailer is permitted to be drawn by passenger vehicles. Provisions are made relative to cars of higher tare weight running previous to the regulations coming into force.

ROADS AND POWER REQUIRED

ROAD wagons can be compared with no other method of transportation, being a class of themselves. Locomotives, using a permanent track, cannot come under the same category, inasmuch as they rely simply upon adhesion to the fixed rails, and do not, as a rule, ascend more severe gradients than one in fifty. With what is required of a road wagon this is almost a negligible factor. In short, for locomotives the track is levelled as far as possible to suit the best running conditions, whilst the motor wagon must be designed to take the common roads as they exist. We can only speculate as to what the newer forms of road locomotion may bring about in the way of improvements in the method of construction of the roads and reduction of the gradients of the same.

In considering the question as at present appertaining, it is essential that the pressure per square inch of road contact must be as low as possible, in order to reduce damage to a minimum. It is obvious that as we now find our roads a wide tyre would not be in contact for more than one-half its width, owing to the uneven surfaces and the excessive camber given for water falling. In extreme instances — as for example on what are usually designated petrified kidneys, found in many Lancashire towns— then it resolves itself into merely a series of point contacts.

For ease in running a large diameter of wheel has undoubted advantages over a small one, but motor-wagon builders are met with the difficulty of the height of the existing loading platforms. The width of a vehicle is restricted to a maximum of 7 ft. 6 in. To encroach upon this limit would be to curtail the available carrying platform area to such an extent as to put such a vehicle out of competition with horse haulage. Small wheels with the platform overhanging are perforce, therefore, to be used for this country; but for the colonies and other countries where no restrictive limits are imposed, larger and better-suited wheels are fitted.

We must not be too severe upon the engineers responsible for our present roads, as for the purposes of the traffic for which they were required they were sufficient, and motor-wagon users cannot hope for radical improvements in road construction to make them satisfactory for weights created by newer forms of transport all at once. It is simply unfortunate that many of our existing roads by no means satisfy the needs of heavy motor traffic, but as the volume of the newer methods of road transport increases, the authorities responsible for our roads must give heed to the altered requirements. Certainly the borough engineers and surveyors are showing a commendable acknowledgment of the conditions which must be brought about to cope with the future exigencies. More toleration is gradually being extended to the movement by public bodies. The conviction in the public's mind that motor traction is becoming a permanent factor for commercial and passenger facilities, and as such must be provided with good roads, will surely call for some system of standardization in construction of roads under departmental government control in order to meet modern requirements.

The macadam roads as now constructed have certainly suffered severely from the extraordinary traffic of heavy road vehicles. Some of such—being of a gross load of 10 tons with two-thirds of this load on the driving-wheels, and having a total width of tyre of 20 inches—have caused a good deal of damage; but the increased tyre width called for by the 1905 Board of Trade Regulations will to a great extent do away with this. But it is not only a question of the damage sustained by the roads, but by reason of the faulty construction of the roads themselves, or perhaps we should say their unsuitability to such traffic, much wear and tear and damaged mechanism results to the vehicles, and this is a point of view to be carefully considered by motor-wagon builders. It is abundantly evident that to enable heavy vehicles to take all roads the worst form of construction found is the one to be considered. This form (for main roads) may be said to be macadam, and the pressure per square inch of tyre contact must be based upon this; and such being the case, for the best results the pressure is out of proportion to what is needed on paved roads. It is difficult to estimate exactly the economic value of good roads to a community. The fact is universally admitted that it is great. The maintenance of roads becomes to users of an extreme type of vehicles (by reason of weight) of supreme importance, appealing to them with a force of unexampled intensity; and it must needs be, therefore, that whatever efforts are exerted, politically or otherwise, to bring pressure upon the authorities should be engineered and energetically prosecuted by builders and users alike. In the Motor Van and Wagon Association we have an organization with this end in view, and already much fruit has attended their united efforts.

A little consideration will show that a satisfactory solution of suitable roads is not to be found by chance, but requires careful study, not only of local conditions, but of certain fundamental principles. The mutual action of roads and road vehicles for various users ought to be studied for both paved and metal roads. In pavements, each stone is of a shape individually to resist the weight of the wheel without any perceptible movement. In macadamized roads, on the contrary, the conditions are constantly changing. The mode of construction is responsible for this—the depth of sand by which the pressure is spread over a large enough surface of the subsoil is not sufficient to prevent it getting out of shape. However great the rainfall may be, heavy motor traffic is quite unaffected on good pavements. If, however, the pavement is badly maintained so that the surface becomes irregular or its paving-stones become too rounded, in addition to the jolts and shocks which are so fatal to the preservation of the mechanism of the vehicles, the surface then constitutes a serious obstacle to heavy traffic. Although 20 in. total width of tyre for a gross load of 10 tons is more than sufficient for a motor wagon working on good pavements, yet it is by no means sufficient when working on macadamized roads. The result of numerous experiments has shown that to convey a 10 ton gross load tyres having a combined surface of 32 in. will not injure the road, but, on the contrary, acting in the nature of a roller, improve the surface. Taking the best practice in steam road rollers, weighing from 12 to 17 tons in working order, and assuming that two-thirds of the weight is carried on the driving wheels, then the pressure per inch in width of tyre varies from 5 to 6½ cwt. Assuming, further, that we have a wagon having a gross weight of 10 tons, with driving wheels 10 in. wide, steering wheels 6 in. wide, and with load distributed in the same way, we get 6½ cwt. per inch of tyre.

With the degree of hardness of the macadam road the amount of power required varies. When very dry and hard the power is practically the same as is required (under all conditions of weather be it noted) with granite setts. The author has often observed in wet weather, that when travelling with a gross load of 10 tons at a speed of 6 miles an hour on setts, that the amount of steam required to keep up that speed was very small indeed. On the same road, where the surface was macadamized, it was difficult to keep up a speed of 4 miles an hour with full steam.

The constitutive elements in metal roads are of small dimensions and have not the surface displacement to resist pressure in the same way as regular and comparatively large blocks, nor can they, as in the case of setts, mutually help one another. The foundation and top layers together form a thickness which is oftener than not insufficient to prevent the subsoil from having to bear so heavy a pressure that it gets out of shape ; and, again, when much rain has fallen, the binding material loses all cohesion and the road becomes a mass of movable stones. The shallowness of the metal and the displacement of the stones transmit to the subsoil a pressure too great for its stability, and hence it gives way. When this is the case the roads continually present an inclined plane in front of the wheels, and thus largely increases the rolling resistance. Engineers are agreed that for this class of road during the rainy season the rolling resistance may be trebled to what it is during fine weather. This is one of the most unfavourable conditions for mechanical propulsion, for it necessitates the motive power being not only capable of a short maximum effort, but a continual one which may be three times greater in wet weather than in fine, unless one is content to curtail the speed.

There has been a considerable amount of controversy on the speed of heavy motor wagons and the amount of damage done by excessive speeds. Unfortunately for the builders, the damage—of which nothing is said by the public authorities—has, as before

stated, not been one-sided. It is incorrect to say that the damage
to the roads has been sustained by reason of the excessive speeds
—rather the contrary. To stand on thin ice is dangerous, though
when passed over quickly that danger is lessened. It is the same
with heavy vehicles on soft macadam roads. It is by reason of
the heaviness of the roads in wet weather and their bad maintenance that the speed of heavy vehicles is reduced, and the
" period " for sinking is increased as the speed is decreased. No
macadam road is homogeneous, and when travelling on a practically level surface the speed of the wagon varies considerably.

On close examination it will be found that the depressions
caused by the road wheels are very unequal. The rut made may

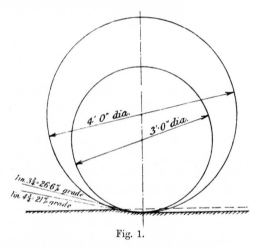

Fig. 1.

apparently be but slight, and one is inclined to give the matter no
further consideration. Fig. 1 shows how deceptive ruts are.
The gradients ascended are shown by wheels 3 ft. and 4 ft.
in diameter.

Wheel diameter.	Gradient 1 in. rut.		Gradient 2 in. rut.		Gradient 3 in. rut.	
2 ft. 0 in.	... 20·7 per cent.	...	29·1 per cent.	...	37·5 per cent.	
2 ,, 6 ,,	... 18·0	,,	... 25·8	,,	... 33·3	,,
3 ,, 0 ,,	... 17·0	,,	... 25·0	,,	... 31·3	,,
3 ,, 6 ,,	... 15·0	,,	... 22·5	,,	... 27·5	,,
4 ,, 0 ,,	... 14·1	,,	... 19·1	,,	... 25·0	,,
4 ,, 6 ,,	... 13·4	,,	... 18·7	,,	... 24·0	,,
5 ,, 0 ,,	... 12·5	,,	... 17·5	,,	... 22·8	,,

The following results, compiled from various authorities, are instructive as indicating the traction effort required under various conditions of surface.

On rails or plates	5·16 lb. per ton.
Asphalte or hard wood . . .	12·24 ,,
Macadam	30·60 ,,
Loose gravel	. 140 to 200 ,,
Sand	400 ,,

And with different tyres as follows (comparatively) :—

Iron	60 lb. per ton.
Solid rubber	60 ,,
Pneumatic	45 ,,

In a paper read by the author in 1899 before the Liverpool Self-propelled Traffic Association he showed that it was necessary to provide a lifting power on the wheel tyres of one-sixth of the total weight of the vehicle, and, when climbing a 1 in 10 gradient, 16 B.H.P. was mentioned as the suitable power in dealing with a vehicle having a gross weight of 10 tons and a ratio of gearing between the countershaft and the road wheels of 28 to 1 with a tare weight of 3 tons. In addition to the gradient we must allow for continually climbing a rut of 1 in. deep on soft or muddy roads, the inclination of the latter depending upon the size of the driving wheels. According to the diameter of the driving wheel so does the curve "hump" itself to meet the road. The gradient incline added to the rut inclination gives the total to be provided for by the power. It is a case of providing a certain "dead lift" in the first place, and the B.H.P. is according to the rate at which we can keep the dead lift going.

If we take the weight of the vehicle complete with the height it is lifted in a given time, making, of course, a sufficient allowance for the friction of the road, the whole thing can be worked out in foot-pounds per minute. A gear capable of forcing any practicable hill would have to be equal to a theoretical lifting power of one fifth of the vehicle. All these points must, of course, be treated relatively and not arbitrarily. The work to be performed is the dominant consideration. Builders turning out standard vehicles must so construct them that they will run on any practical road and in the worst condition thereof regarding weather.

Assuming that we have a vehicle weighing 12 tons, an engine with a piston speed of 500 ft. per minute and a slow-speed gear with a ratio of 20 to 1 for a speed of 2 miles an hour, then

$$12 \text{ tons} = 26{,}880 \text{ lb. lifted } \frac{10 \cdot 560 \text{ ft.}}{6} = 26{,}880 \text{ lb.} \times 1760 \text{ ft. in } 60$$

minutes, which, per minute, would be $\dfrac{26{,}880 \times 1760}{60} = 788{,}480$

foot-pounds per minute $= \dfrac{788{,}480}{500 \text{ piston speed}} = 1576$ lb. average

pressure on the pistons. This would give 1 mile an hour on an incline of, say, 1 in 10, the difference between that and the 1 in 6 provided being lost in friction.

We will take it another way. Say we have 2 miles to travel in one hour up a 1 in 10 gradient, and the gear and road friction make this equal to 1 in 6.

Total load to be lifted $= 26{,}880$ lb. through $\frac{1}{10}$ of 2 miles in 60 minutes; and to provide for doing $26{,}880$ lb. through $\frac{1}{6}$ of 2 miles would be equivalent as regards piston area, through the gearing, of $\frac{1}{10}$ of 2 miles. Then we have $26{,}880$ lb. lifted

$$\frac{10 \cdot 560 \text{ ft.}}{6} = \frac{26{,}880 \times 1760 \text{ ft.}}{60 \text{ minutes}} = 788{,}480 \text{ foot-pounds per minute} =$$

$$\frac{788{,}480}{33{,}000} = \text{roughly } 24 \text{ H.P.}$$

Therefore an engine giving 25 per cent more power, say 30 H.P., would, under normal conditions of working, be powerful enough for ordinary purposes.

The following is a simple means of quickly arriving at "miles per hour" or "ratio" between engine and road wheels.

C = Circumference of road wheel in "feet."

S = Speed of vehicle in "miles per hour."

R = Revolutions of engine "per minute."

r = Total ratio of gearing, e.g. between engine shaft and driving wheels.

To ascertain the "*ratio*" between the engine and driving wheels, the speed of vehicle and the number of revolutions of engine having been fixed—

$$r = \frac{R\ C}{88\ S}.$$

To ascertain "*miles per hour*," revolutions of engine and ratio between engine and road wheels having been fixed, then

$$\text{Miles per hour} = \frac{R\ C}{88\ r}.$$

BOILERS

IT is questionable if any other branch of engineering presents so many difficult problems as the design of steam road wagons, and the generator for these may be said to be the *bête noire*. Not only must it be light, but it must be able to withstand forcing, excessive vibration strains, and often unskilled usage. The demands are also constantly changing to meet the road resistance.

Various types of boilers are in use and many others have been discarded. The commonest form is the cylindrical vertical fire tube with the tubes partially submerged. The objections raised against this class are that the tubes must expand unequally and deteriorate more in the steam space than where water-covered. The author has had nine years' experience of this type, and is much inclined to the belief that these objections, if not exactly chimerical, are much exaggerated, and, granting an element of truth in the objections, yet the simplification of construction, ease of dismounting, safety, and general " fool-proofness " more than counterbalance any disadvantages. When made with a central feed and with the top tube plate and furnace crown connected, this makes undoubtedly the strongest form of boiler. Ordinary fire doors in this class of boiler have given trouble by reason of the unequal contraction of internal parts due to sudden inrush of cold air, and they are now mostly dispensed with. Trouble was also experienced with the clinkering doors, although this was not the fault of an ordinary fire door, as such, but mainly due to the faulty design of the door ring. In place of the fire door the fire bars are now dropped, which effectually overcomes previous objections. An important point in favour of the vertical fire-tube boiler is the steady water level maintained under all conditions of working. The railway locomotive engine, on the other hand, runs under very different conditions of gradients to the road steam wagon; and it is conceivable, therefore, that in stiff gradients or steep declines, where a locomotive type of boiler is fitted, the water is thrown to one end of the boiler, leaving the tubes at the other end, perhaps, only partially or wholly uncovered.

The vertical water-tube boiler as used by Messrs. Thornycroft, having an upper and lower drum connected by tubes without a clinkering door, has also given very good results.

The De Dion, with various modifications, is used with economical results as regards fuel consumption, but requires more than ordinary attention if this efficiency is to be maintained.

There is, apparently, a strong tendency to revert to locomotive patterns varying in details, e.g. firing on the top, side, or end; using drop fire bars, and dispensing with a clinkering door. One maker has gone back to the "coffee-pot" type of loco boiler, viz. where the barrel of the boiler is filled with water and the fire box taken well above the barrel, the point of difference being that the firing is done through a central shoot passing through the steam and water space. Three old-established firms have in their 1905 models included wagons fitted with loco type boilers, although for rough or colonial work vertical boilers still seem to be fitted and preferred.

There are also several modifications of the fire-tube type (vertical) having totally submerged tubes.

It is a most difficult matter to design a boiler to meet all conditions, and no one type can be said to be the best. Each have their own advantages and disadvantages, and are suitable for certain classes of work. The aim of builders must be to design the boiler to meet the majority of the conditions; and, therefore, a boiler that is simple in construction and having plenty of space between the tubes; easy of access and with practically uniform working water level, will probably be found the best all round. The locomotive type is favoured for good level roads, and, having these conditions, it is economical; but for all-round machines not operating in restricted and favourable areas or for colonial use the vertical form has so far held its own. Of course a great objection to the loco type is the amount of space occupied, which considerably curtails the available carrying area, which, in comparison with horse-drawn vehicles, is already poor enough. If the same carrying space is given, an extended wheel base and strengthening of frame, etc., is necessary, and the size becomes somewhat unwieldy. One firm certainly gets over this latter difficulty by putting their boiler across the frame in front.

LANCASHIRE STEAM WAGON Co.

Fig. 2 shows a section of an oil-fired fire-tube boiler designed by Mr. James Sumner, of the Lancashire Steam Motor Co., in 1894. Seventy-five of these boilers have been sold for lawn mowers and steam road wagons. Reference to the illustration will show that the boiler consists of an outer shell in one piece,

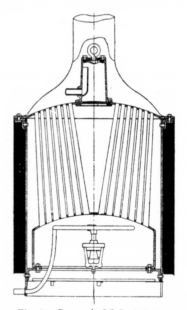

Fig. 2.   Sumner's Oil-fired Boiler.

provided with an outside angle ring at the top, to which is bolted the top tube plate. Near the bottom of the shell is an inside angle ring, to which is bolted the fire box, connected to the top tube plate by 198 taper copper tubes $\frac{3}{4}$ in. 16 B.W.G. at the top and $1\frac{1}{4}$ in. diameter at the bottom. There are no stays of any kind in this boiler. The steam is collected in a dome situated in the chimney stack. To disconnect, all that is necessary is to break the top and bottom joints and lift the inside of the boiler out by means of the eye bolt in steam dome. The drawing shows the design used in the 1898 and 1899 Liverpool trials, and was then and is now—so far as the author is aware—the most economical oil-fired boiler yet designed. During the said trials the consumption of ordinary petroleum was at the rate of ·56 gallon per vehicle mile with a 4 ton load. The burner is of the "fair ground" type, and is cheap and efficient in work, but very noisy. The evaporative performance is very high, being 12 lb. of water with 1 lb. of petroleum fuel. But even with oil at 6d. per gallon against coke at 12s. per ton, the latter is three times cheaper, so that, except under special circumstances, oil cannot compete.

Fig. 3 is a sectional elevation of the Leyland fire-tube central-feed type, designed by Mr. Henry Spurrier, jun., in 1900, and since used by his company (Lancashire Steam Wagon Co.) as their standard pattern. The boiler consists of an upper and lower shell bolted about midway. The fire box is contained in the lower shell. The central firing shoot acts as a stay between the upper tube plate and the fire-box crown. The tubes are screwed and beaded over in the fire box, and expanded in the top plate—the latter so as to allow of expansion to take place here rather than at the furnace crown. The whole length of the tubes can be exposed readily by disconnecting the upper shell. The tubes are of tough seamless steel, and the space between them is unusually large to admit of easy cleaning. Attached to the top tube plate is a steam drier, the steam entering it through a few small holes at the opposite side to the outlet, and, by passing between the tubes, gets well dried. With a 200 lb. pressure it might be conjectured that the top and middle joints would not constitute a good mechanical job; but in practice they give no trouble whatever when made with good asbestos, which may be used several times, provided that black lead on the top and red lead on the under side are applied. Central firing obviates the necessity of often opening the fire box, and hence the trouble of leakage (owing to contraction of the metal by the sudden admission of cold air experienced with the ordinary fire door) is overcome and the life of the tubes materially increased.

This boiler, fitted with copper tubes, proved to be very economical at the 1901 Liverpool trials.   It was somewhat small,
having only 76 sq. ft. of heating surface and 2·5 sq. ft. of grate
area.   The declared working pressure was 225 lb. per sq. in.,

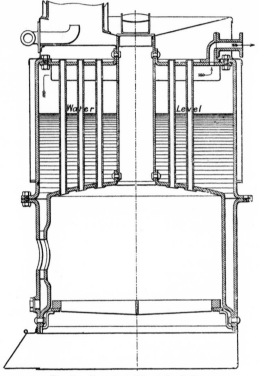

Fig. 3.   Spurrier's Fire-tube Boiler.

yet the average pressure on four days' running—167 miles—
was 212 lb. per sq. in.   The following is the fuel and water
consumption :—

Fuel per gallon of water, L.B.S.	Gallons of water per vehicle mile.	Lbs. of coke per vehicle mile.	Miles per hour.	Miles covered.
1·74	6·2	11·38	6·0	40
1·80	6·5	11·7	6·3	42·5
1·96	6·9	11·5	5·8	41·0
1·81	6·3	11·4	6·2	43·7
Average . 1·82	6·47	11·13	6·07	Total 167·2

T. TOWARD & Co., NEWCASTLE-ON-TYNE

Messrs. T. Toward & Co. have for several years made a speciality of boilers for steam wagons. Fig. 4 is an external view and Fig. 5 a sectional elevation of their Class A Rapid Light High-pressure Boiler.

This consists essentially of two tube plates connected across by water tubes at their lower portion, and above by a single large

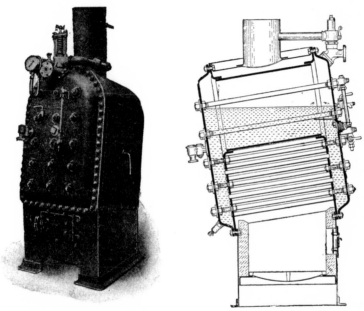

Fig. 4. Toward's "A" Boiler.　　Fig. 5. Sectional Elevation of Toward's Boiler.

tube which acts as a steam drum. Embossed and flanged covers or end doors, suitably stayed, form the water pockets into which all the tubes open. These are inclined, to promote rapid circulation in a definite direction. By removing the end doors easy access is gained to the tubes for cleaning or repairs. The top and sides of the boiler are enclosed with a casing of light steel, with smoke-box doors at the sides. The fire box is also formed with a light steel casing extending below the fire bars and forming the ash pit and support for the fire grate. The fire box is lined with brick.

The following particulars are furnished by the makers:—

Size No. 4. Heating surface, 60 sq. ft.; grate area, 3 sq. ft.; evaporation per hour, 560 lb. Consumption of coke per hour, 72 lb. Dimensions: height, 4 ft.; length, 2 ft. 4 in.; width, 1 ft. 10 in. Weight, 810 lb. The tubes are of solid cold-drawn steel, 84 in number, 1 in. diameter.

One hour's test made to determine the capacity of the boiler: water evaporated, at a pressure of 190 lb. per sq. in. above atmosphere, 615 lb.

		P.M.	
Lighted up coke fire at		1.18	
Water boiling from all cold		1.32	= 14 mins.
10 lb. steam per sq. in. at		1.36	= 18 ,,
20 ,, ,, ,, ...		1.38	= 20 ,,
50 ,, ,, ,, ...		1.40	= 22 ,,
100 ,, ,, ,, ...		1.41	= 23 ,,
150 ,, ,, ,, ...		1.42	= 24 ,,
180 ,, ,, ,, (safety valve lifted) at		$1.44\frac{1}{2}$	$= 26\frac{1}{2}$,,
Trial began with strong blast in chimney at		1.46	
Finished at		2.46	

The makers claim that the boiler does not prime even when worked under a forced draught equal to 4 in. of water.

Fig. 6 is an excellent view and Fig. 7 a sectional elevation of the "Toward" Class B High-pressure Boiler. This boiler has a water-jacketed fire box and tubes running from the front to the back wall. The front and back water spaces are carried upward and connected by a large, single water tube, which acts as a water and steam drum. The shell is thus rectangular in form, open at the top and the upper part of the sides, the remainder being all water spaces (excepting the grate and fire door), having the walls stayed in the usual manner. The distance from the fire-grate level to the bottom of the tubes is not less than 11 in.

The leading particulars are as follows :—

No. 4 boiler. Heating surface, 65 sq. ft.; grate area, 3 sq. ft.; height 4 ft. by 2 ft. 4 in. long by 1 ft. 10 in. broad; weight,

about 810 lb.; weight of water in boiler, 250 lb. The following
test is reported by the makers:—

P.M.

Coke fire lighted at	3.0
Water boiling from cold, temperature 42° F., at .	3.15 = 15 mins.
10 lb. steam per sq. in. at	3.19 = 19 ,,
20 ,, ,, ,, ...	3.22 = 22 ,,
50 ,, ,, ,, ...	3.24 = 24 ,,
100 ,, ,, ,, ...	3.25 = 25 ,,
150 ,, ,, ,, ...	3.26 = 26 ,,
200 ,, ,, ,, (safety valve lifted) at	3.27 = 27 ,,
Trial began at	3.40
Finished at	4.40

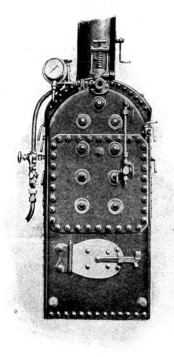

Fig. 6. Toward's " B " Boiler.

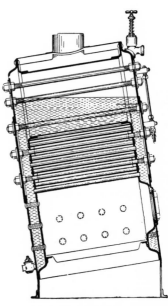

Fig. 7. Sectional Elevation of
Toward's Boiler.

Water evaporated equals 758 lb. at a pressure of 200 lb. per
sq. in. Consumption of coke, 108 lb., say 7 lb. of water evaporated and raised to 200 lb. pressure per lb. of coke.

The steam discharged is given as " dry," and this the author can confirm.

By comparing the evaporative performance of this boiler with Class A (practically the same capacity) the results of the improved pattern are apparent. This is no doubt due to the extra and valuable heating surface of the fire box. In Class A the fire-brick lining is not satisfactory, and in Class B the fire door has been the cause of some trouble. This has now, however, been dispensed with and a very simple form of shoot arranged at right angles to the door shown in the illustration.

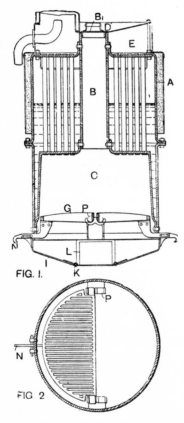

FIG. I.

FIG 2

T. COULTHARD & Co., PRESTON

Fig. 8 is a sectional elevation and plan of a fire-tube boiler of the central-feed type designed by the author, the chief point of difference being the absence of the clinkering hole. The object aimed at was to obtain equal expansion in the water drum. To do this the fire bars were designed to drop and also the ash pan; but these can be operated independently of one another. This was probably the first fire-tube boiler fitted with drop bars; and this feature has since been incorporated by the majority of manufacturers using vertical boilers.

Fig. 8.   Coulthard's Boiler.

THORNYCROFT

In the 1898, 1899, and 1901 Liverpool trials Messrs. Thorny-croft used a water-tube boiler (see Fig. 9). This consists of an upper and lower drum connected by tubes and centrally fed. Some difficulty, by reason of sudden dropping of temperature by the inrush of cold air, was experienced when using a side clinker-ing door, but drop fire bars were subsequently used which success-fully overcame this disadvantage. One hundred and sixty-eight straight steel tubes, $\frac{7}{8}$ in. external diameter, were employed. The top vessel was built up of two $\frac{5}{16}$ in. steel rings, riveted at their

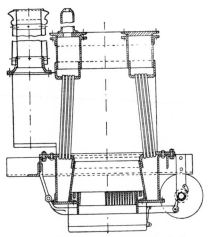

Fig. 9. Thornycroft Water-tube Boiler.

lower edges to an annular steel channel $\frac{1}{2}$ in. thick. Three plates, viz. one tube plate $\frac{5}{8}$ in. thick and two rings $\frac{5}{16}$ in., composed the lower vessel. Steel covers were used for both chambers, secured by bolts in the case of the top and studs for the bottom. The tubes were 1 ft. 11 in. long, and their mean inclination $1\frac{1}{16}$ in. to 1 ft. The heating surface was 77 sq. ft.; the grate area $2\frac{1}{3}$ sq. ft., and total weight $13\frac{3}{4}$ cwt. The boiler is built for a safe work-ing pressure of 200 lb. per sq. in. and hydraulically tested to

350 lb. per sq. in.   The water drum was enlarged; and, with clinkering holes eliminated, the boiler has given very good results. Steam is raised quicker than with a fire-tube type, but, on the other hand, the fluctuation in the water level is comparatively very great.

The difference in design in locomotive types consists almost entirely in the modes of firing. (1) Firing through the top, without clinkering door and using drop fire bars; (2) through the top, with separate door for clinkering; (3) at the side, using same opening for clinkering; (4) at the end, using same door for clinkering; (5) at either side, with separate clinkering door. For the reasons expressed when dealing with vertical boilers and the experience gained therewith, the first method is probably the best.

Fig. 10 shows a section of a new locomotive boiler used by Messrs. Thornycroft. The central feeding tube passes through

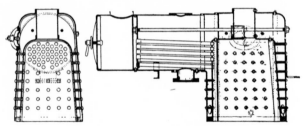

Fig. 10.   Thornycroft Locomotive-type Boiler.

the steam and water space, and at the same time serves as a means of securely connecting the furnace crown to the outer shell. The heating surface is 57·5 sq. ft. and the grate area 4 sq. ft. The safe working pressure is 200 lb. per sq. in.

FODEN & Co.

The "Foden" machine, fitted with a locomotive Type 2 boiler, ran well in the War Office trials at Aldershot, December, 1901. The following is the fuel and water consumption :—

Fuel per gallon of water, L.B.S.		Gallons of water per vehicle mile.		Lbs. of coke per vehicle mile.		Miles per hour.
1·8	...	7·56	...	12·60	...	5·2
1·75	...	6·80	...	11·9	...	6·3
1·76	...	7.03	...	12·3	...	5·9
1·60	...	7.98	...	12·76	...	6·09
1·65	...	7·30	...	12·04	...	6·9
1·15	...	8·06	...	9·26	...	6·03
1·70	...	6·88	...	11·69	...	6·2
1·57	...	7·53	...	11·822	...	6·4
Average . 1·62	...	7.39	...	11.809	...	6·12

Total miles traversed = 258.

THE STRAKER STEAM VEHICLE Co.

This boiler is a modification of the De Dion et Bouton type.

Figs. 11 and 11A are sectional elevation and plan respectively, from which the construction will be easily understood. The design is based on the radial and concentric principle. There are four concentric shells, each pair of which form an annular water space, which are connected by a nest of radial tubes, the interstices between them forming the boiler flue. The hot gases generated in the furnace duly pass up through the flue space between the tubes, which are placed to give complete baffling, so that by the time the hot gases reach the smoke box the bulk of the heat is exhausted. The fuel is fed through a central chute. A damper is fitted at the chimney base for controlling the draught, and additional regulation is obtained by removing lid on firing hole. The extreme shortness of tubes conduces to freedom from incrustation. Muddy deposits can be removed through four mud

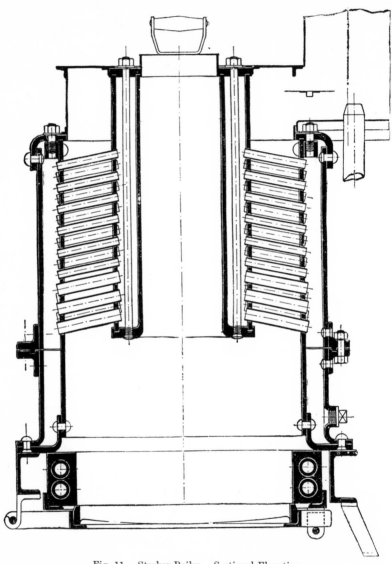

Fig. 11.   Straker Boiler.   Sectional Elevation.

holes in the outer shell. For internal opening up the dome is removed, exposing the entire nest of tubes.

The fire bars are arranged well below the water-line, and the space between is made up with a casting containing a coil through which the exhaust steam passes. In this type of boiler the

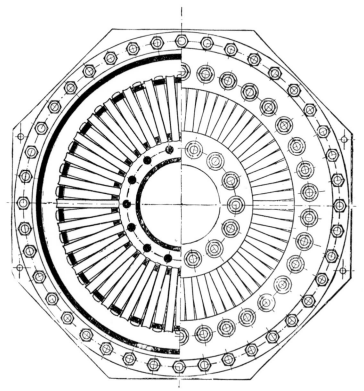

Fig. 11A. Straker Boiler. Plan.

temperature of the gases are low; hence the necessity for heating the exhaust to lessen the amount of visible vapour, and from this point of view it is scarcely so successful as other types; but the fact remains that the boiler is very economical from a fuel point of view; the weight, number of parts, difficulty in cleaning, and cost of production, however, militate against it.

THE YORKSHIRE PATENT STEAM WAGON Co., LEEDS

Fig. 12 shows this company's patented boiler. It is on the locomotive principle as regards the fire box, but is provided with two short instead of one long barrel, and is fixed across the front end of the frame immediately over the front axle. Two sets of tubes connect the fire box with the chambers

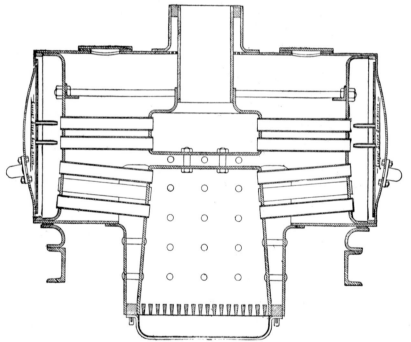

Fig. 12.   Yorkshire Steam Wagon Co.'s Boiler.

at each end of the barrels, and return tubes convey the gases to another chamber at the base of the chimney. There are 32 1¾ in. steel tubes in the fire box and 28 tubes leading from the smoke boxes to the chimney base. All the tubes are totally submerged, which is an excellent feature. The products of combustion travel equally on the right and left from the fire box to the smoke boxes, hence, by the velocity of the exhaust steam, they are induced to travel through the second row of tubes to the base of the chimney. The number of exhaust jets in each end is 14 and the diameter of the orifices $\frac{1}{4}$ in. To clean the tubes, all that is necessary is to unlatch the smoke-box doors at the ends, when they are all disclosed. The fire door is arranged above the foot plate, as the design does not well lend itself to a central-tube feed.

The working pressure is 200 lb. per sq. in.; heating surface, 53·3 sq. ft.; grate area, 2·65 sq. ft. The length of the boiler is 4 ft. and the diameter 2 ft. The shell plates are of mild steel, and the fire box and stays are of Lowmoor iron.

The consumptions given by the makers are very low: about 11 lb. of gas coke per vehicle mile with full load and 20 lb. of water evaporated per square foot of heating surface. The design of the boiler is such that a high duty should be obtained and the consumption of fuel should be low. The arrangement of the boiler across the frame admits of providing only a fuel bunker of very small capacity.

JAMES ROBERTSON & SON, FLEETWOOD

The boiler used by the above firm on their motor wagons is of a somewhat novel construction, with many good points to commend it. Fig. 13 is a sectional elevation, and Fig. 13A a part section plan of the boiler. The tubes are laid horizontally, the object aimed at being to have all the tubes totally submerged and to make use of the products of combustion to heat a greater portion of the outer shell. Immediately above the fire box the fire tubes are arranged radially from the feed chute. The products of combustion pass through these tubes to the outer casing, which is lined with asbestos, and thence to the chimney. The engine exhaust, after passing through the feed-water heater, enters the connexion (B) above the level of the furnace crown, the pipes being bent round the boiler shell and coupled to the top connexion (B), above which is the reduction

nozzle at the base of the chimney. The firing is effected through
the centre opening, a lid (not shown) being used to close the
aperture when not feeding. In practice the hot gases do not
escape through the feeding hole, though there will be a tendency

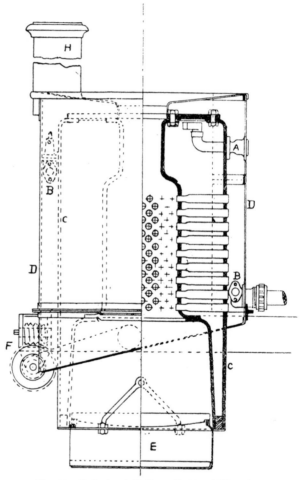

Fig. 13.   Robertson's Boiler.   Sectional Elevation.

for the products of combustion to pass to the chimney the easiest
way, which is on the chimney side. Since the water level is
above the top row of tubes the danger of fire-box heating is
eliminated. It is not a difficult matter to clean the fire tubes

internally, as this can be done by simply removing the outer casing or employing a steam brush. To clean the tubes externally the top plate must be removed and a scraper used. The

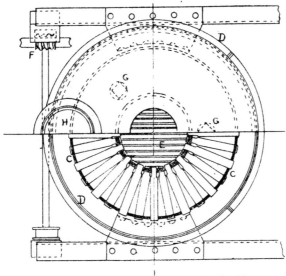

Fig. 13A. Robertson's Boiler. Part Section Plan.

steam is collected from the extreme top of the boiler (A). Baffle plates above the fire tubes are not used, though their use would ensure dry steam entering the steam pipe; but' on the other hand, they would interfere with the external cleaning of the tubes. The clinkering door is dispensed with, a system of dropping the fire being used. The ash pan (E) supports the fire bars, the pan and bars being raised and lowered by means of worm gearing operated by a hand wheel in front of the vehicle (Fig. 13B).

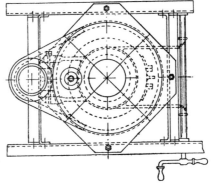

Fig. 13B. Bar-operating Gear—Robertson's Boiler.

This boiler is simple, and there is no reason to doubt its ability as a good steam raiser.

JESSE ELLIS & Co., Ltd., MAIDSTONE

Fig. 14 is a sectional elevation of the "Ellis-Balmforth" boiler, with which the wagons manufactured by Messrs. Jesse Ellis and Co., Ltd., were equipped for several years. By referring to

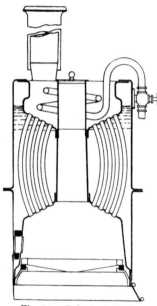

Fig. 14.   Balmforth Boiler.

this illustration it will be seen that the fire tubes connecting the furnace crown to the upper plate are curved and totally submerged. The object of this curvature is to allow for expansion and contraction without disturbing the tube ends. The ordinary working level is well above the fire tubes. Steam is taken to the uppermost part of the boiler, and then passes through a coiled pipe on its way to the main steam valve. The feed water is fed into the lower water chamber, which is the correct place.

A clinkering hole is arranged at the side, and the ordinary fire bars are fitted. It will be observed that the central feeding tube is tapered, having its largest diameter at the bottom. This is a good feature, and will reduce the danger of clogging up the firing tube, which can happen in the case of a perfectly cylindrical tube.

For their latest wagons the above boiler has apparently been superseded by a loco-pattern boiler fired from the top.

THE "HERCULES" MOTOR WAGON Co.,
LEVENSHULME, MANCHESTER

The boiler manufactured by this firm see (Fig. 15) and fitted to their steam road wagons is of the totally submerged vertical fire-tube class, its essential variance being that the products of combustion after passing through the vertical fire tubes enter the

smoke box, and from thence pass through a series of inclined
diagonal tubes, and then to the chimney. By this arrangement
of inclined tubes the water is prevented from " swishing " up, and
should undoubtedly largely militate priming. A large heating
surface is secured, and every part subject to the hot gases is
in direct contact with the water, or entirely surrounded thereby, so that the temperature can only assume the degree of the
water with which it is in contact, and equal expansion is largely

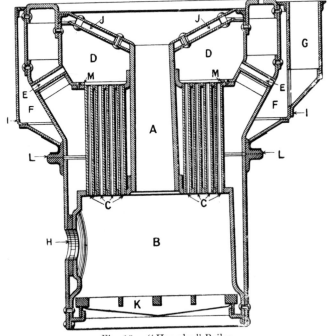

Fig. 15.   " Hercules " Boiler.

secured. The general method of employing drop fire bars is not
employed, an inspection and clinkering door being arranged in the
side. If this were cut out and dropped fire boxes used, the claim
to any unequal expansion would be more fully substantiated.
The sudden inrush of cold air on opening a side door must set up
a severe contraction. Theoretically one would think this to be a
negligible quantity, yet the practical fact remains that pronouncedly
better results have been secured by the substitution of drop fire
bars for side doors in otherwise identically designed boilers.

BOILER FEED PUMPS AND BOILER
FITTINGS

THE arrangement of the best methods for feeding the boiler; the check valves; pressure gauges and other boiler attributes are matters that require very careful consideration, and depend upon the special design and *tout ensemble* of the mechanism of the wagon, so that it is only possible to exemplify by patterns in use by reputable manufacturers.

Automatic feeds have been tried with varying success. The system usually adopted is a ram pump worked off the engine by means of reduction gear, some makers preferring to regulate the suction, and others to regulate by means of a bye-pass, the suction being constant and the amount of water not required being returned to the water tank. The universal practice is to draw the water from the tank and force it through a coil arranged in an exhaust silencer; the exhaust steam from the engine playing round the coil constitutes a feed-water heater previous to the water being delivered to the boiler, by which time the water is raised to about 180° F. Where the amount of water allowed to enter the pump is regulated so that an approximate constant speed of supply is obtained, then the water is forced to the boiler at practically a uniform temperature; but when the regulation is effected by means of a bye-pass, and the surplus water is permitted to return to the supply tank, then the coil feed-water heater is subject to great variations of temperature, which necessarily retards steam raising. For this reason the method of regulation of the amount drawn by the pump would seem to be commendable rather than a bye-pass control.

A very simple form of ram pump is shown in Fig. 16. The valve box and the pump barrel are separate castings. Duplicate suction and delivery valves are employed. The pressure when delivering is about 400 lb. to the sq. in. on the ram, and this is taken through two bolts. Free access to the stuffing boxes is secured by this arrangement. The speed of the pump is practically constant irrespective of the speed of the vehicle.

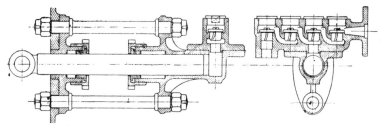

Fig. 16.   Boiler Feed Pump.

Fig. 17 shows a sectional elevation through glands and plunger of the boiler feed pump employed by Messrs. T. Coulthard & Co. and designed by the author. In this pump the ram is protected

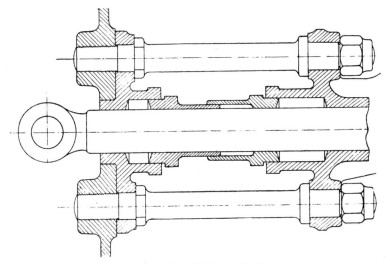

Fig. 17.   "Coulthard" Boiler Feed Pump.

from dirt, whilst the packing glands are always exposed to view and easily available. The suction is regulated so as to give as near as possible a constant feed. The second motion shaft of the transmission from which the pump is driven is always in gear, so that the speed of the vehicle has little bearing on the speed at which the pump works.

For auxiliary feed supply injectors, or small steam pumps, are used. A considerable amount of trouble has been caused by the steam pumps being of too small a construction, necessitating running them at excessive speeds. Then, again, they were of too

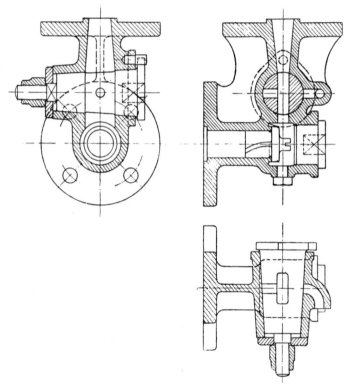

Fig. 18.   Single Check Valve.

light a construction and not intended to work at 200 lb. per sq. in. pressure. Providing the pump is large enough to supply the boiler, and of sufficient strength in construction, there is no reason why a steam pump should not be thoroughly satisfactory for auxiliary feed purposes.

The exhaust from the safety valves should be taken to the water tank, which will thus act as a preliminary "feed-water heater";

but this raising of the temperature interferes with the working of an injector, since it is impracticable to fix an injector so as to allow the water to run to it.   The ram pump and also an auxiliary steam pump can be arranged so that the supply runs to the pumps, and in this way admit of using water of a fairly high temperature.

The position of the check feed valve is one calling for discriminating judgment.   It is not good practice to deliver the feed

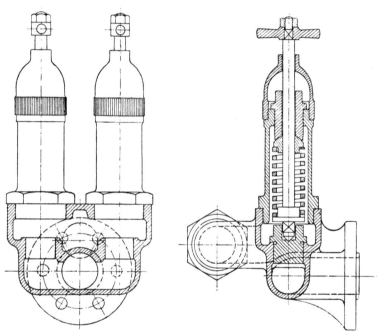

Fig. 19.   Double Safety Valve.

into the boiler at one place unless there is an internal pipe encircling the fire box.   Independent suction and delivery pipes ought to be used whether an auxiliary steam pipe or injector are employed.

A very good design of check feed valve is shown in Fig. 18. The object aimed at is to enable communication with the boiler to be shut off for examination of the check valve whilst the boiler is under pressure.   Should the attendant omit to open the plug valve under ordinary conditions a burst in the pump or pipes would ensue. In the design shown this danger is overcome by arranging a bye-pass in the plug which signals to the attendant by issuing a jet of water.

It is advisable also that double safety valves should be fitted to boilers used for heavy motor wagons. In view of the necessarily limited weight permissible, the high pressure used and the constant variation of temperature attending their use, this is only a reasonable precaution, and some of the boiler insurance companies make it a *sine qua non* to their acceptance of the risk of insurance.

Fig. 19 shows a design of a double safety valve which has acted perfectly in long use. Simplicity is its keynote, and adjustments can only be made by taking the cap off. One valve is set slightly in advance of the other, and this arrangement makes the action very sensitive.

Steam gauges, being subject to much vibration, should be fitted with a test cock on the syphon in order to give constant communication with the boiler.

WHEELS

THE form of construction of wheels best adapted for motor wagons has apparently proved a problem of no mean calibre, for this and a really satisfactory form of boiler have proved the two most persistent obstacles to overcome. One is inclined to think at times that we are too easily satisfied, and that in our designing we are superficial, resigning ourselves too readily to accept the "recognized and useful" as the "right and inevitable"; inclined to adhere too rigidly to grooves in which we have long run, instead of carefully studying the underlying right principles, having the courage of our deductions, and boldly striking out on new lines. In the construction of wheels for motor wagons this trait is most noticeable, and only quite recently has any decided inventiveness been displayed in designing a heavy motor wheel *per se*, rather than mere adaptations of forms of wheels used for other vehicles, but eminently unsuitable, as results have proved, for the new conditions encountered by extra speed, weight, and direct driving of the wheels. Necessitous changes from past practice are required both in nature and degree, but the relative bearing one to another was not in the first place appreciated or understood. It may have been that the novelty attending the application of power and mechanism for propulsion of vehicles on common roads was so fascinating as to absorb our whole attention, to the exclusion of any thought to fit the older essentials to the newer requirements. Perhaps the Liverpool Trials were the first clear indication of the neglect in design of suitable wheels, for in the first and second series, though the wagons in their mechanical aspects were satisfactory to a great degree, yet the wheels all round were a source of unending trouble.

In the first models we find ordinary lorry wheels employed; in 1899 the "gun carriage" and "traction engine" were intro-

duced; and at the present time we have a diversity of forms—
traction engine, plate, cast steel, gun carriage, and composite.

Fig. 20 shows a traction type of wheel. This form has given
fairly good results on macadam roads; but on "cobbles" and
setts, found so extensively in the north of England, only very
indifferent results have been obtained. Until the regulations of
1905 the use of section strips were illegal. Wheels of this
pattern were therefore perforce to be made with a single smooth
tyre, which soon began to spread and caused the rivets to loosen.

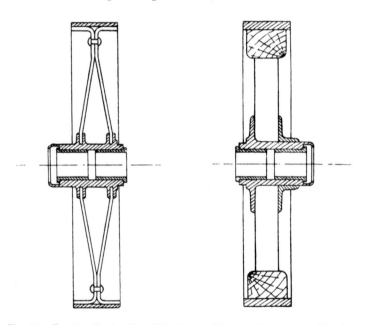

Fig. 20. Traction Engine Type Wheel.   Fig. 21. Gun-carriage Wheel.

The spokes cast in the hub soon worked loose also—more especially when the drive was taken through the spokes.

Fig. 21 shows what is perhaps the commonest type prevailing,
but not necessarily the best, viz. the "gun-carriage" pattern.
In the early stages of the industry much trouble was caused by
not using well-seasoned wood, for what was considered sufficient
seasoning in wood used for like purposes in construction of wheels
for other vehicles—two years in the open—should, from the
author's experience, be increased to at least four years for use in

heavy motor work. The woods found most suitable are English ash for the felloes and English oak for the spokes. When it was the practice for the drive to be taken directly through the hub, or a ring or triangular attachment to the spokes, these had to withstand the whole propulsive force and strain. Since the driving is now taken direct to the felloes of the wheels this strain is better allocated, and spoked wheels have met with a much greater measure of success.

Great care must be exercised in building up this wheel, and the periphery of the felloes should be turned so that the tyre—which must be of the best cold-drawn weldless steel—fits easily. The thickness of the tyre should be $1\frac{1}{8}$ in., and only wheels which have been tyred by hydraulic pressure are capable of standing up to their work. The pressure applied by a hydraulic tyre machine can be varied up to a maximum of 1 ton per sq. in. The right pressure to employ depends upon the strength of the wheel. After the wheel has been tyred, the centre is accurately bored to receive the hub. The author has seen wagons which have run for four years with the woodwork in good condition. The tyres require, of course, renewing after $1\frac{1}{2}$ to $2\frac{1}{2}$ years' work, according to the nature of the roads traversed and the amount of actual work performed. The nearer the final drive is transmitted to the periphery the longer will be the life of the wheel. In all side chain-driven machines, therefore, where the terminal drive is a chain wheel fixed to the road wheel the former should be attached as near the tyre as possible. If attached to the spokes they will soon work loose, and experience has dictated, and all makers now design, by different means, that the terminal drive shall be borne by the felloes where the spokes are of wood. Whatever attachment, however, is used, the holes for this attachment will not come into alignment after a wheel has been retyred. Hence new

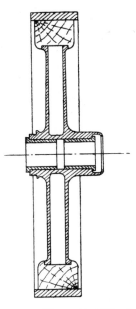

Fig. 22. "Composite" Wheel. Section.

holes after retyring must be bored, and in this wise the strength
is lessened.

The mathematical accuracy of construction and fitting makes
the "gun carriage" an expensive wheel to build, whilst the
number of loose parts necessary are not in its favour. It was
with the object of getting over the latter objection more especially, and at the same time of obtaining a better method of fixing

Fig. 23.   Spurrier's Composite Wheel.   Elevation.

the chain-wheel support, that led **Mr. Henry Spurrier, jun.,** to
design, in 1901, the composite wheel shown in Figs. 22 and 23.
This wheel was in the first instance made in channel section, but
modified subsequently to the section shown in the illustration.
The essential element of this wheel consists of a single casting,
combined steel hub and spokes, the latter fitting into the usual
ash felloes shod with cold-drawn steel tyres. The object, of

course, in arranging wood between the steel centre and the tyre is that all the advantages of a "gun-carriage" wheel are obtained —the wood acting more or less as an elastic buffer absorbing the road shocks—whilst the number of loose parts is reduced to a minimum, and a much better arrangement of attaching the chain ring is secured, the strength of the steel spokes being sufficient to take the drive, which separate wooden spokes fitting into the felloes and hub formerly could not stand. Retyring can also be effected more readily, and without detriment to the wooden felloes. Four years of actual running have shown these wheels to stand remarkably well, and this type of wheel is being adopted by several other leading makers of steam wagons and motor buses. It is alike suitable for home and colonial use, which is an advantage in manufacturing standard machines.

Figs. 24 and 25 show a very good type of steel plate wheel, which is well suited for colonial requirements. It will be seen by reference to the drawing that the hub is fixed between two dished plates, and the chain-ring drive is attached to the hub between the arm spaces.

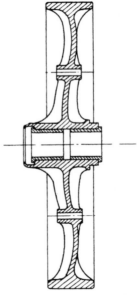

The 1905 regulations permit of separate tyre plates being used for the tread, the plates being separated by parallel spaces to be disposed throughout the outer surface of the tyre, so that nowhere shall the aggregate amount of the space in the course of a straight line drawn horizontally across the circumference of the wheel exceed one-eighth part of the width of the tyre. Now with all wheels shod with plates "spreading"

Fig. 24. Steel Plate Wheel. Section.

takes place, the period varying with the road conditions, and although the space between the plates may be only one inch, "spreading" soon causes the plates to lift. Smooth-faced tyres with a polished surface are naturally more liable to skidding or slipping; but from a mechanical point of view a weldless tyre hydraulically applied must always prove more reliable and longer lived, tending, as it does, to bind and keep firm the whole wheel.

A considerable number of wooden-shod wheels have been from time to time designed, principally for winter use to get over the disadvantage of slipping on snow and greasy roads. The fault of all these seems to have been that the width of the wooden

Fig. 25.   Steel Plate Wheel.   Elevation.

tyres have been corresponding to iron wheel treads, and hence, owing to the great difference in the nature of the materials used, the wooden wheels have soon come to destruction. Roughly speaking, had these wooden tyres been made of double the tread width, much better results would have been obtained.

A wooden-tyred wheel of some promise is now manufactured by Mann's Patent Steam Cart and Wagon Co., Leeds. This consists of a cast steel inner wheel with a polygonal rim, to which is bolted beech-wood blocks or segments with grain end on. To prevent the wood splitting, plate segments or clamps with slot holes in them are bolted against the sides of the blocks and the rim of the inner cast steel wheel. The ends of the plate segments are a sufficient distance apart to allow them to be drawn towards the centre of the wheel, so that they will not come into contact with the road as the wooden blocks become worn down, but by occasional adjustment they may be kept at

Fig. 27.   Mann's Patent Winter Wheel.

a suitable distance from the tread or outside of the wheel. Upon the flat surface of the polygonal rim the foot of the wooden blocks is bedded and held by radial bolts; the joints between the adjoining blocks are radial, so that they constitute a thick wooden shoe round the whole of the steel centre; and, to better enable them to take the side thrust, the sides are, as before stated, clamped between the steel plates.

The wheel is shown in Fig. 27, from which the construction and action will be readily understood.

In summarizing the practical deduction to be drawn from

existing designs of wheels for heavy vehicles, and the considerations involved in the production of what may more nearly approach the ideal requirements, the following points must be carefully considered and incorporated.

As weight carriers, the wheels must be sufficient to carry the load designed for; be able to do this successfully for a long period without undue tiring of the metal or other material of their construction, and to withstand the undue and constantly varying jolts and strains of different classes of roads, whether in good or poor maintenance order.

The speed at which vehicles are driven under the circumstances of improper roads is excessive, and the wheels must be able to withstand the worst conditions of road and maximum speed with maximum loads, and there must be an amount of resilience or elasticity in the construction to ensure that the amount of jolting shall not conduce to breaking up, and thus give an unreasonably short life.

The wheel must be capable, either through its hub, attached ring, or felloe, to transmit the power, whilst its lateral strength must be such as to withstand extraordinary side pressure, as in the case of running or skidding against a kerb.

The widths of tyres set out by the 1905 regulations are, of course, a minimum, but from the builder's point of view the diameter must be such that its width will allow it to run on and not cut into the road surface and thereby absorb power; and the tyre must not (as in said regulations is sufficiently guarded), apart from sufficient width, damage the road.

The most difficult problem attending wheels, in view of protection from damage to roads, is to prevent the tyres from spinning round and not biting the ground sufficiently to propel the vehicle under frosty or greasy conditions. This applies to iron tyres only, of course, for the upkeep of solid rubber or pneumatic tyres for heavy vehicles makes their cost prohibitive.

Agreeable with other qualifications the prime cost should be low, although, in view of the importance of the subject, this is the last consideration that must weigh in the design of a satisfactory wheel.

The 1905 regulations will necessitate some modifications in design, and so far as artillery wheels are concerned, for the larger vehicles at any rate, the difficulty in obtaining suitable wood of the required section may bar their use. Wheels with elastic tyres or non-metallic resilient tread are classified apart, and hence an impetus may be given to the design of wheels of other forms. Indeed, in the "Gare" wheel (Fig. 28) such a departure is seen. This is most interesting and of it something good may be expected. Wedge-shaped wooden blocks, dovetailing as it were one with another, are placed tangentially to the hub. In order

Fig. 28. Gare Patent Resilient Wheel.

that the load may be distributed over a large area, a band or bed of soft rubber is interposed between these central blocks and the tread blocks, which are of **V** shape. By this arrangement there is no excessive pressure acting upon the rubber, and hence its elasticity is not impaired with long use. The tread blocks themselves are saturated with a special rubber solution to render them impervious to wet or affected by heat. Steel bands round the face wheel hold the tread blocks together, though in so wise as not to restrict their working, while still distributing the pressure over a large portion of the rubber.

The road wear is taken only partially by these tread blocks, the holding steel bands coming also into contact with the road. Renewal of these after wear is easy, though it is claimed that the amount of wear obtainable is very much more than might be conjectured.

Any shock or jolt is intercepted before it can be transmitted to the axle by the mode of construction, whilst a really astonishing degree of resilience is secured. The fact that it is silent and said to be non-slipping are also important points.

The "Boulton" wheel has been applied to traction engines, but as its construction requires a large diameter, it is very heavy; and as it is also expensive to manufacture, it is not applicable to ordinary road wagons, except for colonial use or War Office requirements (to which the regulations give latitude). Considerable resilience is secured with a steel wheel having a wide tyre, and it overcomes any slipping tendency. The construction may be said to be a typical traction-engine wheel, but what would be equivalent to the felloe is a casting round the circumference, of which two rows (generally) of holes are spaced alternately. Blocks of wood, metal cased, are loosely inserted into these holes with their outward ends protruding, and retained in position by bolts and springs. A practically wooden tyre is thus formed which successfully moderates the hammering of the setts or protuberances of the road. The blocks naturally require renewing from time to time, but this is an inexpensive matter, the advantages gained more than compensating.

The weldless steel tyres, being of a ductile nature, by reason of the road impacts and hammering effect of setts, etc., have not proved all that could be desired, as they wear out quickly or roll out thin. Cast steel, being tough yet non-ductile, is not subject to the drawbacks attending weldless steel; and cast-steel wheels of a proper mixture—care being taken that it is not brittle—have shown that the wear from contact with the road surface is very little indeed.

A new wheel has latterly been put on the market by Mr. Stagg which possesses some good qualities. This consists of a cast steel rim having on its under side pockets cast integral with it, into which ordinary wooden spokes are forced and bolted. This is shown in Fig. 29. The other ends of the spokes are held by the hub, which is of a patent design; the arrangement being such that any spoke may be detached or replaced at will without disturbing or affecting any other part of the wheel. The outer ends of the spokes are made very large to give a wide bearing surface against the steel rim, and this is an advantage. With ordinary artillery wheels with wooden felloes there is only a narrow shoulder to receive the end thrust, whereas in this wheel the

Fig. 29. Stagg Wheel.

whole end—indeed, purposely enlarged—is utilized. The wooden spokes act, as in the composite wheel, as anti-vibrators to absorb the road shocks, and the benefit of a cast-steel rim, little affected by wear, is also secured. The advantage of being able to renew the parts at will is certainly an improvement on wheels cast in one piece, because damage to the latter necessitates an entirely new wheel.

It is impossible to more than briefly touch upon the requirements, present practice, and lines of future advancement. The subject is one of considerable magnitude, and to but mention the devices or attempts made to surmount the real or apparent disadvantages would not materially help to the solution of the problem, which has up to the present successfully baffled the ingenuity of designers; but, undoubtedly, immense strides have been made within the past few years, and before long we may expect some really remarkable results, possibly in the direction of the introduction of a resilient agent interposed between the road contact and the wheel of the vehicle to isolate the mechanism, and thereby reduce excessive repairs, and what is a strong objection by municipalities and others, the excessive vibration and noise set up. A little more money expended upon wheels to effect this result would be a material saving in the long run, and be the means, more than any other, by which the life and satisfactory commercial working of heavy road wagons would be enhanced.

BRAKES

THE design of a suitable brake for heavy vehicles is an important matter, and the following requirements are essential.

(1) It should be capable of holding the machine when descending a gradient at three miles an hour when fully loaded and with the engine out of gear. Several serious accidents have occurred owing to the driver attempting to change speed from fast to slow when ascending a hill and "missing" the gear. In this event the driver is absolutely dependent upon the brakes; and if they are not applied immediately the wagon will get out of control. In such instances the brake should, of course, have been lightly applied before endeavouring to change gear.

(2) It should be capable of retarding, or bringing to rest, a vehicle equally well when running in either a forward or backward direction. Brakes having the property of effecting this are termed "double-acting," although many of the brakes so named are only so partially, being more effective in one direction than another. Modern practice tends to the use of brakes in which the frictional surfaces are of metal, as, when in continual use down long inclines, any form of lining is liable to overheat or char.

(3) Another important consideration in brake design is the effect caused by unequal retardation of the road wheels, resulting in making the vehicle particularly liable to skid or side-slip—especially if the roads be greasy.

As the duty of a brake is to dissipate the energy or accumulated work stored up in the moving mass of the vehicle, we must first ascertain what this is before we can calculate the power and strength required in any portion of the brake gear.

Let W equal the weight of the vehicle in pounds, and V the velocity in feet per second. Then

$$\text{Accumulated work in foot-pounds} = \frac{W\,V^2}{2\,g}$$

where g represents the acceleration due to gravity $= 32 \cdot 2$ ft. per second. Take for example a vehicle weighing, when loaded, 8 tons, and running at a speed of, say, 3 miles an hour.

From the above formula we have—

$$\text{Accumulated work} = \frac{8 \times 2240 \times \left(\dfrac{3 \times 5280}{3600}\right)^2}{2 \times 32 \cdot 2} = 5370 \text{ foot-pounds.}$$

In calculating the brake power required it is essential to take into consideration the co-efficient of friction between the tyre of the wheel and the road surface. This necessarily varies according to the condition of and the material used in the construction of the road, but for ordinary macadam and steel tyres we may take it as being about 0·4. As the brakes are applied only to the rear or driving wheels of the vehicle, we must next ascertain what proportion of the total load is carried by these wheels. Let us assume, for example, this to be 5 tons. Then the minimum distance L in which the vehicle can be brought to rest is found by the formula—

$$L = \frac{\text{Accumulated work.}}{\text{Coefficient of friction} \times \text{Weight carried by driving-wheels in pounds.}}$$

Taking our example, we have—

$$L = \frac{5370}{0 \cdot 4 \times 11,200} = 1 \cdot 2 \text{ ft.}$$

Then the braking power required on the tyres of the road wheels $= \dfrac{5370}{1 \cdot 2} = 4475$ lb.; one-half of this being applied to each road wheel.

The shoe brake is applied by various makers in an indifferent manner, apparently without regard to the strains set up by the application of the leverage. Fig. 30 shows a form of this brake very commonly used, and consists of blocks or shoes A pivoted to hanging levers B, whose fulcrums are on the frame of the vehicle. These levers are coupled together by means of a crossbeam, to which the operating rod C and bell-crank lever D is attached. The latter is operated by means of a vertical screw-down hand wheel.

One of the objectionable features of this brake is that all the braking strains are transmitted through the road wheels on to the axle, and, as an end pressure, on to the springs of the vehicle. The swinging movement of the springs on their carrying levers requires that it shall be taken up before the full power of the brake can be applied. As this is considerable, the process of applying the brake to its maximum power is needless loss of time and detracts from the absolute control necessary in emergencies, where loss of time might involve unknown consequences. Fig. 31 shows a form of double-acting shoe brake designed by the author, which, besides being much more powerful, is quicker in operation, and entirely overcomes the objections found in the previous example. The vertical hand-wheel shaft

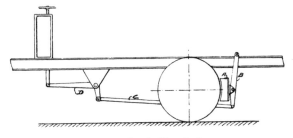

Fig. 30.   Single Shoe Brake.

transmits motion through a pair of mitre wheels to the horizontal shaft A; this shaft is coupled, by means of a universal joint, to a right- and left-hand screw B, working in a bracket C bolted to the rear axle. To the two nuts (which are caused to move equally and in opposite directions by the screw B) are coupled the crossed rods D. These rods when the brake is applied are all in tension, and, as will be readily seen, exert an equal pull on all the four brake shoes, relieving the springs, axle, and other parts of the vehicle of all strains, and whilst acting against one another make what may be termed a "self-contained" brake, taking whatever power is applied equally upon all four shoes. This system of brake can also be worked easily by steam or hydraulic power. If, in place of the right- and left-handed screw, a cylinder be substituted, then by admitting steam, water, or oil—as the case might be—to the centre of the cylinder, and thus forcing out in opposite directions two pistons, to which the crossed rods coupling up to the brake shoes could be attached, the same action would be effected.

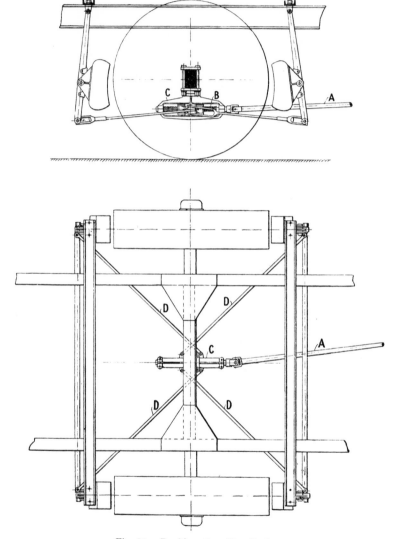

Fig. 31.   Double-acting Shoe Brake.

Figs. 32 and 33 represent single and double-acting band brakes. The diameter of the brake drum in this type being much less than that of the road wheels, the pull on the brake rods will have to be increased in inverse proportion to the diameter of the road wheels to the brake drum.

In the single-acting type, assuming the road wheels to be 30 in. diameter, the brake drum 15 in. diameter, and taking the total pull as before, viz. 4475 lb., we then have $\dfrac{4475 \times 30}{15} = 8950$ lb. total pull required, or 4475 lb. on each brake band.

One of the weak points in the band brake as usually fitted are that it is exposed, and being attached to the driving wheels of the vehicle soon gets clogged with dirt, oil, etc., causing undue

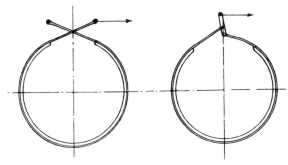

Figs. 32 and 33.   Single and Double-acting Band Brakes.

wear and greatly affecting the frictional properties, and consequently the efficiency of the brake. To overcome this the Lancashire Steam Motor Company designed the brake shown in Fig. 34. It is an internal expanding shoe brake, acting on the inside of sprocket wheels. In the illustration, A represents the sprocket wheel and brake drum, B is a fixed arm centred on the axle. On one end of this arm are hinged the brake shoes, which are of cast steel, and made channel section to receive a number of hard-wood blocks, which can be easily renewed when worn. Attached to the other end of arm B is a rod C, coupling to the frame of the vehicle. The operating lever D and short toggle lever E are fulcrumed on a stud F fixed in arm B, the

toggles and brake shoes being coupled together by links G.   In
this brake the pressure on the two shoes is equalized.

A similar form of brake to the last is sometimes used, wherein

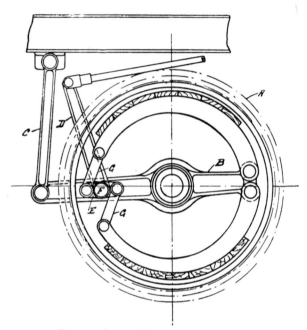

Fig. 34.   Internal Expanding Shoe Brake.

the brake shoes operate on to an external drum, but this lacks
the valuable property of protection from dirt, etc., which the
internal system possesses.

STEERING

THE type of steering most commonly employed on motor
wagons is that known as the "Ackerman," so named after
the inventor, who introduced this system as long ago as 1818.

The essential principle underlying this method consists in

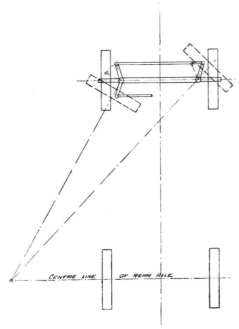

Fig. 35.   Ackerman Steering.

replacing the pivoted fore-carriage of an ordinary vehicle having
one axle for the two wheels by two pivoted arms on which the
road wheels rotate.   To obtain correlative running of the two
wheels, and to ensure that there is only a rolling action on the
tyre of the wheels when turning, Ackerman introduced inclined

arms or levers, coupled together by means of a rod (see Fig. 35).
By this means the axis of the two steering wheels, when swung
round on their pivots, can be made to converge at a point on the
axis of the two rear or driving wheels. Each steering wheel is
thus turned through an angle corresponding to the radii of the
curves through which it is travelling.

This system of inclined arms and coupling rods permits of
their being placed either in front or in the rear of the axles of

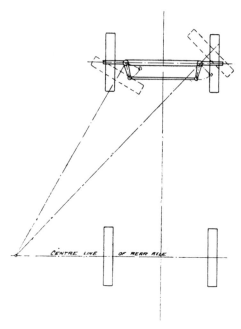

Fig. 36.　Ackerman Steering.

the steering wheels, according to convenience in design. When
placed in front (as in Fig. 35) the arms are inclined away from
each other. If in the rear (as in Fig. 36) they are inclined
towards one another.

It is evidently of first importance in this type of steering that
the point of support of the wheel shall be as near as possible to
the pivot above which the axle arms turn. The chief reason for
this is that the line of stress, coming more directly under the
pivot, greatly reduces the bending effect or leverage on the pivot.

thus enabling the steering wheel to be more readily turned, and also lessening the shock on the steering gear produced when the steering wheels come into contact with any obstruction on the road. The Ackerman principle, however, though giving very good results in practice, only imperfectly fulfils the conditions required for road traction, inasmuch as it can only be absolutely correct in two positions, viz. (a) that in which the wagon is running in a straight line; and (b) at some particular angle, dependent on the choice of the point on which the axis of the road wheels converge. To overcome this inaccuracy Mr. Davis has produced a modification (see Fig. 37) which gives absolutely accurate movement of the steering wheels for every angle in which the vehicle may travel. Looking at the figure, A1, A2 is the centre line of the driving wheels; B1, B2, the centres of the steering wheels in straight position; C1, C2 is a line the same distance in front of B1, B2 that A1, A2 is behind. If the centre line of the levers D1, D2 are always caused to intersect in the line C1, C2, then the axes of the wheels will themselves always intersect in a corresponding point on the line A1, A2. This is effected by causing the levers D1, D2 to be actuated by means of guides, the coupling-rod of which is also guided by means of brackets on the fixed axle.

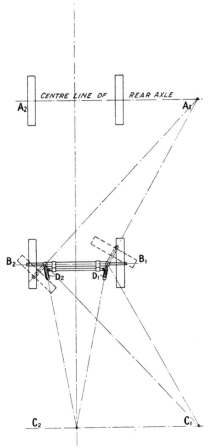

Fig. 37.
Davis' Improved Ackerman Steering.

In travelling over rough and uneven roads, it is desirable that the steering wheels should be able to accommodate themselves to the varying character of the track on which they run without disturbing the frame or body of the vehicle. There are several designs in use for accomplishing this end, one of which is illustrated in Fig. 38. To enable the steering wheels to retain their

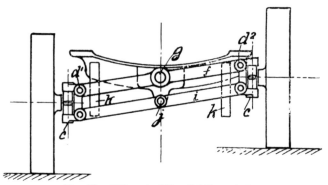

Fig. 38. "Hercules" Parallel Front Axle.

vertical position on the ground in this arrangement a parallel motion is ingeniously arranged. Referring to the figure, f is a pair of double-armed levers pivoted at g, a corresponding pair of levers or links i are pivoted at j. On the ends of these levers brackets (d^1 and d^2) are hinged, these brackets in turn carrying

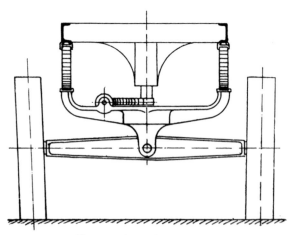

Fig. 39. Centre-lock Steering.

the pivots. (c) about which the short axle arms and road wheels turn. Plates (k) are used to steady the links (f and i).

In Fig. 39 is shown the centre-lock system of steering, found more frequently in traction engines than in the steam lorry. When used for the latter type of vehicle the fore-carriage is turned by means of a worm gear, the wheel of which is secured to the central pivot. A greater amount of angle or "lock" can be obtained with this method than in the Ackerman principle; as, if so desired, there is nothing to prevent the fore-carriage swinging round through a complete circle, whilst in the other systems described the "lock" is limited, firstly by the angularity obtained in the short steering levers, and, again, by reason of the road wheels coming into contact with the springs of the vehicle. This latter feature usually determines the amount of lock obtainable in any of these forms of steering, and in practice is usually about 35°.

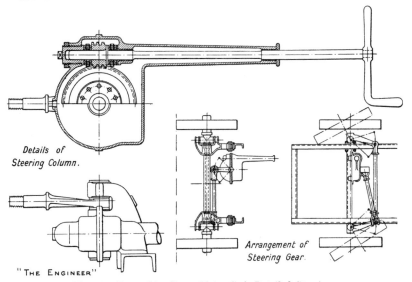

Details of Steering Column.

Arrangement of Steering Gear.

"THE ENGINEER"

Fig. 40.   Lancashire Steam Motor Co.'s Detailed Steering.

Coming now to the methods employed in operating these different forms of steering, we find that the one most frequently met with is the worm and wheel gear. Details of this gearing are shown very clearly in Fig. 40. In the best practice—absolute reliability at all times being essential—the gearing is enclosed in a dust-proof and oil-tight casing. The worm is of hardened steel, and gears with a phosphor-bronze cut wheel or sector. Ball thrust washers are employed on each side of the worm, and adjustment is provided for wear.

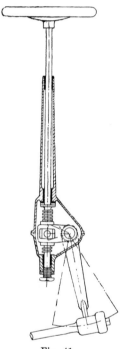

Fig. 41.
Screw and Nut Steering Gear.

Another gear sometimes used, but found more frequently on the lighter class of road vehicles, is the screw and nut type in Fig. 41. It is difficult to see why this gear is not more generally employed, seeing that the working surfaces are much larger than in the worm and sector; the gear consequently developing less back-lash (a most objectionable feature in any steering gear), and has therefore a longer life than can possibly be expected in worm and wheel gearing. If a **V**-shaped thread be used, by splitting the nut and tightening up the screws when wear has taken place, an efficient means of adjustment is provided.

Owing to the independent movement which takes place between the frame of the vehicle and the axle, as well as the change in direction of motion in the levers, universal joints are advisable for connecting the lever on the steering column to that on the axle arm.

In the heavier type of road vehicle an irreversible form of steering gear is absolutely essential, i.e. one in which any opposing force met with on the road wheels cannot transmit return movement through the steering gear. Both the above-mentioned gears are equally irreversible.

SPRINGS

THE type of spring used for heavy motor vehicles is apparently exclusively confined to the semi-elliptic, as in railway and tram practice.

The usual method of carrying is by means of two brackets which slide in **V**-shaped blocks attached to the frame as regards the rear springs, the front ones being held by one fixed and one sliding bracket; preferably these brackets being made from a dissimilar metal to the frame, say phosphor-bronze.

The following formulæ by D. K. Clark are reliable for railway practice or for vehicles travelling on rails, but the author has found it necessary to modify this for road vehicles.

E = Deflection in $\frac{1}{16}$ in. per ton load.
S = Span, when loaded, in inches.
N = Number of plates.
B = Breadth in inches.
T = Thickness in $\frac{1}{16}$ in.
L = Working strength, or load in tons.

Then—

$$\text{Deflection} \quad = E = \frac{1 \cdot 66 \times S3}{B \times T3 \times N} \quad (1)$$

$$\text{Working strength} = L = \frac{B \times T2 \times N}{11 \cdot 3S} \quad (2)$$

$$\text{Number of plates} = N = \frac{1 \cdot 66 \times S3}{E \times B \times T3}$$

When extra thick back and short plates are used, they must be replaced by an equivalent number of plates of the ruling thickness prior to the employment of the formulæ (1) and (2). This is found by multiplying the number of extra thick plates by the cube of their thickness (in $\frac{1}{16}$ in.) and dividing by the cube of the ruling thickness.

In place of the above formulæ the author has found it advisable to substitute the following for road vehicles :—

$$\text{Deflection} \quad = E = \frac{1\cdot 7 \times S3}{B \times T3 \times N} \quad (1)$$

$$\text{Working strength} = L = \frac{B \times T2 \times N}{12\cdot 3S} \quad (2)$$

$$\text{Number of plates} = N = \frac{1\cdot 7 \times S3}{E \times B = T3}$$

Copy of Autographic Record of Test—Exact size as taken.

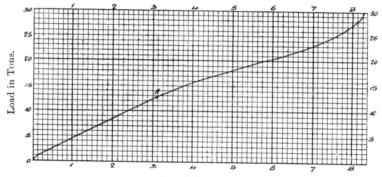

Actual Deflection in Inches.

N.B.—The Elasticity of the Spring remained perfect up to $12\frac{1}{2}$ Tons, as shown at A, Permanent Set remaining after tenth application of a Load of 10 Tons.

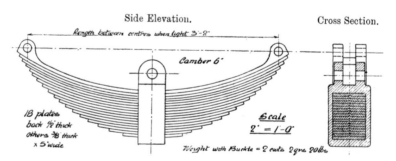

Side Elevation.　　　　　　　　　　　Cross Section.

Safe Load (D. K. Clark) $= \dfrac{B \times T2 \times N}{11\cdot 3S} = \dfrac{5 \times 6 \times 6 \times 18}{11\cdot 3 \times 36} = 7\frac{1}{2}$ tons (actually 8 tons).

Deflection per ton of Load up to 10 Tons $= \cdot 23''$.

Fig. 42. Test of Locomotive Spring.

At one time short springs with a large amount of camber were commonly used, but the tendency, both for heavy and light vehicles, is to much extend their length and allow only a small camber—almost approaching the flat when fully loaded. There is no doubt that this gives a much easier riding and smoother spring effect.

The diagram (Fig. 42) shows results of a test made by Prof. G. F. Charnock, of the Bradford Technical College, on a "Buckton" 100 ton testing machine of a standard Midland Railway locomotive spring.

THE LANCASHIRE STEAM MOTOR Co., Ltd.

THE above company were one of the earliest, if not the first, to take up seriously the production of steam road vehicles. In 1896 a steam van was constructed with the idea of competing in the "Engineer" trials in that year at the Crystal Palace. The limit tare weight imposed by the judges was one ton, and this vehicle, which subsequently did a lot of work, exceeded this stipulation; but in the following year the same van secured the only award given by the Royal Agricultural Society of England at Crewe. This machine was fitted with an oil-fired boiler (with a steam pressure of 150 lb. per sq. in.), change-speed gear operated from the driver's seat, two side chains for the terminal drive, and a fixed axle. It is worthy of note that these features have never been deviated from in the company's long and extensive manufacturing.

In 1898 a larger vehicle was built to carry 4 tons, and secured the first prize of £100 from the Royal Agricultural Society of England at the Birmingham trials, and also the first prize of £100 at the 1898 trials of the Self-propelled Traffic Association. The performance of this wagon was remarkable (a summary of details and performances will be found in the Appendix). The tare of the wagon was under 3 tons, as required by the then prevailing law, yet the average load carried was 4 tons at an average speed of 5¼ miles an hour. The consumption of petroleum as fuel was 0·56 gallons per vehicle mile, and the consumption of water 3·4 gallon per vehicle mile, making an official record which, so far as the author is aware, has not been bettered to date.

In 1899 a similar wagon competed in the second series organized by the Liverpool Self-propelled Traffic Association and gained the second prize. This year was the last of the oil firing by this firm, as the trials conclusively showed that it could not compete with solid fuel as a steam raiser in motor wagons.

The following year, 1900, saw the company's 4 to 5 ton coke-fired wagon. This vehicle in the third series of Liverpool trials

Fig. 43.   Lancashire Steam Motor Co.   4-Ton Wagon.

in 1901 gave a meritorious exhibition and was awarded the highest award—a gold medal. The tare of this wagon was under 3 tons; no other vehicle competing came within the legal limit. The average load carried was 4·81 tons; average speed 6 miles an hour, and the total distance travelled was 167 miles. The consumption of water was 6½ gallons per vehicle mile, and the consumption of fuel (coke) 12 lb. per vehicle mile (*vide* Judges' Report).

This vehicle is known as Class B, and in general design, excepting that every part has been strengthened as found necessary by experience, is practically identical with the 1901 model.

Fig. 43 is a general view of the 4-ton wagon. It will be seen by reference to the illustration that the boiler is placed in front of the fore axle, the engine and transmission gear between the two axles, and the water tank behind the hind axle.

Engine and transmission.—The engine is of the compound link reversing type, having high-pressure cylinder bore $3\frac{1}{2}$ in. and low-pressure cylinder $6\frac{1}{4}$ in., both with 6 in. stroke. Stephenson's link gear is used with block piston valves working in renewable liners. An arrangement, operated from the driver's seat, is provided for working both cylinders with steam direct from the boiler, with independent exhaust from each cylinder. No keys are used, all wheels being put on flanges.

Two speeds are provided (see Fig. 44), operated from the driver's seat: fast speed, 5·2 miles per hour; slow speed, 2·6 miles per hour; with an engine speed of 450 revo-

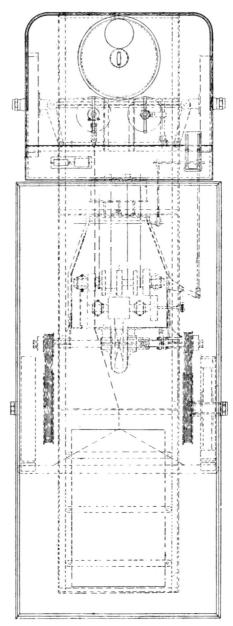

Fig. 44.   Plan of Lancashire Steam Motor Wagon.

lutions per minute. The ratios of gearing between the engine and
road wheels are 10·8 and 21·6 to 1. Two spur pinions of unequal
diameters are attached to the crank shaft. The second-motion
shaft consists of two spur wheels of unequal size on the ends,
and a spur pinion midway between the two spur wheels. This
shaft slides in two bearings, and the spur pinion is of such a
width that it is always in gear with the large spur wheel on the
differential shaft. The compensation gear shaft is hollow from
end to end (see Fig. 45). A bolt is put through this and takes
the end thrust caused by the differential bevel wheels. By
operating a lever under the frame of the vehicle the compensating
gear can be locked if desired by means of an internal clutch.

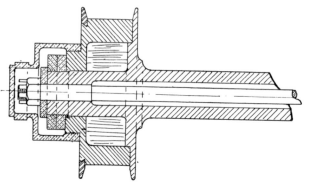

Fig. 45.   Lancashire Steam Motor Co.'s Cushion Drive on
Compensating Gear Shaft.

The drive from the compensating shaft ends is taken to the
road wheels by Renolds' roller chains. A flexible cushioned
chain pinion of the company's patent design is fitted on each end
of the compensating gear shaft. By referring to Fig. 45 it will be
seen that this cushion is obtained by interposing between the
driving and the driven portion of the vehicle four rubber blocks.
The action is as follows:—When power is transmitted to the
shaft, the rubber blocks are compressed until their resistance is
such that the drive is taken up by the sprocket pinions. This
cushioning, coming into play as it does after the engine speed has
been considerably reduced through intermediate gearing, allows
the crank shaft making about a revolution before movement can
take place at the road wheels.

The engine, reduction and compensating gears are all contained in a self-contained casing, which has a three-point support from the frame.

The lubrication of the working parts inside the casing is of the simplest description. The chamber is charged with oil—the amount being fixed by the opening of a test cock on the side of the casing—and all the parts are then running in an oil bath. The cylinders are oiled by a patent sight-feed lubricator with a duplicate system of feed in case of the glass breaking.

Boiler.—The boiler (see Fig. 3) is of the company's well-known

Fig. 46. Lancashire Steam Motor Co. 1906 Pattern.

type designed by Henry Spurrier, jun., in 1900. The heating surface is of 81 sq. ft. and grate area 3·2 sq. ft. Working pressure 200 lb. per sq. in. The quantity of water contained in the boiler up to ordinary working level is 31 gallons ; height of water above furnace crown (working level) is 12 in. The boiler is fed with a ram pump running at practically a constant speed irrespective of the vehicle's speed. Duplicate suction and delivery valves are a feature of this pump, which can be run when the vehicle is stopped. For the auxiliary feed supply there is an injector with independent suction.

The wheels are of the "Leyland" composite pattern (see

article on "Wheels" for details), which are claimed to possess all the advantages of the gun-carriage pattern, whilst dispensing with loose hubs and spokes. The driving wheels are 3 ft. diameter with 9 in. face, and the steering wheels 2 ft. 10 in. diameter with 5 in. face. The tyres are of weldless steel hydraulically fitted.

The company's own type of brakes (see Fig. 34) are fitted.

	Tons	Cwt.	Qr.
The tare-weight of wagon complete is . .	4	11	0
The weight on front axle (light)	2	6	3
The weight on hind axle (light)	1	18	1
Weight in working order, tank and bunkers full—			
Front axle	2	13	2
Hind axle	2	17	1
Total . .	5	10	3
Weight with 4 ton load—			
Front axle	2	18	2
Hind axle	6	12	0
Total . .	9	10	2

General dimensions—Length over all . . . 17 ft. 9 in.
                Width   ,,   . . . 6 ft. 6 in.
                Platform   . 12 ft. by 6 ft. 6 in.

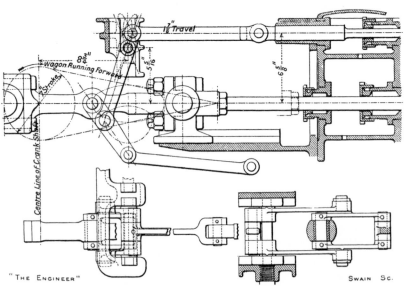

"THE ENGINEER"   SWAIN SC.

Fig. 47.   Lancashire Steam Motor Co.   Engine Valve Gear.

Fig. 46 is an external view of the "Leyland" 5-ton vehicle built to comply with the 1905 regulations, which will deal with 5 tons on its own platform and is capable of additionally hauling a

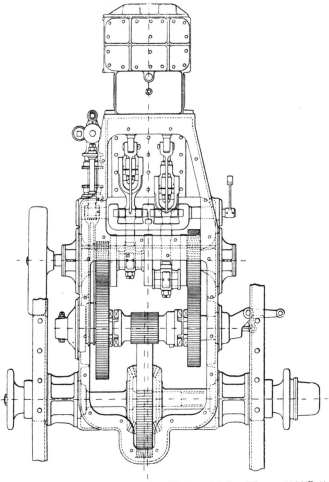

Fig. 48.   Lancashire Steam Motor Co.   Engine of 5-Ton Wagon, 1906 Pattern.

trailer with 2-ton load.   Several improvements are incorporated in this design.

Engine and Transmission.—The engine is compound and fitted with a "constant lead" valve gear with straight link. A diagram of the general design is shown in Fig. 47. The high-pressure cylinder bore has been increased ½ in., making it 4 in., and the low-pressure also increased ½ in., making it 6¾ in. bore. The same length of stroke, viz. 6 in., is retained. The ratios of gearing between the engine and road wheels are 19·4 and 11 to 1, giving speeds of 2·9 and 5·1 miles per hour with engine running at its normal speed of 450 revolutions per minute.

Fig. 48 shows a plan of the engine and gearing. The valves are of the flat balanced pattern working on renewable faces. Unlike the smaller wagon before described, the second-motion shaft gearing runs loosely when the combined sliding clutch and pinion is out of gear with the spur wheel. The second-motion shaft is in reality a

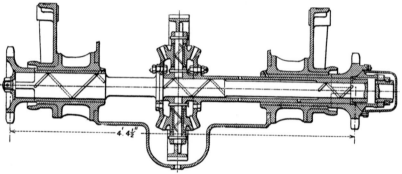

Fig. 49. Lancashire Steam Motor Co. Compensating Shaft.

fixed steel tube with the clutch operating rod working in the hollow. The compensating shaft is clearly shown in Fig. 49. It will be noticed that the main bearings are non-adjustable. The third axle consists of a " Mannesman " tube with practically solid ends. The rear axle has bearings 11 in. long and 3½ in. in diameter, the diameter of the axle beyond the bearings being 4½ in.

The boiler, brakes, and steering gear are the same design as on the smaller wagon.

The driving wheels are 3 ft. 6 in. diameter by 10 in. face, and the steering wheels are 3 ft. diameter by 6 in. face. The tare of this machine is 4 tons 18 cwt.

THE THORNYCROFT STEAM WAGON Co., LTD., CHISWICK AND BASINGSTOKE

This well-known firm were one of the very first to enter upon the manufacture of steam road wagons, and it is largely to them and one or two other equally enterprising pioneers that the general success of them is due. Competing wagons have been entered by Messrs. Thornycroft in all the public trials which have taken place in this country, and have been attended with conspicuous success.

Fig. 50.   Thornycroft 4-Ton Wagon.

The general features of the 4-ton wagon are common to all sizes manufactured by the company, and a description, therefore, of the one will be sufficient (Fig. 50).

Engine.—The engine is of the horizontal compound reversing type with cylinders 4 in. and 7 in. diameter by 5 in. stroke. It has a constant lead, radial valve gear of the company's special design, by which all degrees of linking up may be obtained. The cranks and other moving parts are enclosed in a dust-proof and oil-tight casing, which being partially filled with lubricating oil, provides efficient lubrication by the "splash" system. To facilitate adjustments or examination, a large and easily removable door is fitted to this casing.

At normal speed the engine develops 30 B.H.P.

Transmission.—In some heavier types chains were tried, but have been discarded altogether, as it is stated unsatisfactory results were only secured for the great power required. All the company's vehicles are now fitted with their own patent system of chainless gearing, whereby free motion of 7 in. is permitted between the wagon frame and the driving axle without disturbing

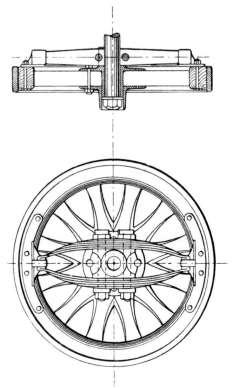

Fig. 51.   Thornycroft Spring Drive.

the steady continuity of the running effort and without any possibility of jump in the gearing.

The first-motion gear wheels are of steel with machine-cut teeth, whilst the drive is transmitted to the differential gear through steel gear wheels with double helical teeth, giving great strength just where it is needed, and also greater smoothness and quietness in running. These gear wheels are of cast steel, unmachined; but in order to obtain true meshing and sweet running they are run together for a time in oil and emery.

Wheels.—Artillery wheels are usually provided, but cast steel and composite wheels are also fitted for colonial or special requirements.

The tyres are hydraulically pressed on the artillery wheels, thus avoiding the charring of the felloes inseparable from the old process of shrinking on of tyres of such size and thickness.

Spring Drive.—By means of a patent spring drive (Fig. 51) the spokes are relieved of all strain, and, in addition, sudden jars to the wheels through bumpy roads and increased speeds are absorbed before reaching the mechanism of the vehicle, thus tending to economy of maintenance and prolonged efficiency. This is an excellent feature, as by this arrangement the shocks are absorbed at once—the springs being interposed at the right place for effecting this—and there is no doubt that this driving system has done much to enhance the reputation of the firm's products.

Boiler.—In general the well-known water-tube boiler of the firm's speciality is employed.

Additional steam space to prevent priming and the substitution of a vertical movable grate in place of a side clinkering door are notable recent improvements. The boiler comprises essentially two annular chambers connected by a series of 168 straight steel tubes $\frac{3}{4}$ in. in external diameter.

The top vessel is built up of two separate rings of $\frac{5}{16}$ in. steel, riveted at their lower edges to an annular steel channel $\frac{1}{2}$ in. thick. The bottom vessel is composed of three plates, i.e. one tube plate and two rings. The tube plate is $\frac{5}{8}$ in. thick and the rings $\frac{5}{16}$ in. The covers of both chambers are of steel, and are secured by bolts, in the case of the top vessel; and by studs in the bottom. The connecting tubes between the two vessels are 1 ft. 11 in. long, and their mean inclination $1\frac{1}{16}$ in. to 1 ft. The heating surface in this smaller size of boiler is 77 sq. ft., the grate area 2·4 sq. ft., and the total weight $13\frac{3}{4}$ cwt. The boilers are built for a working pressure of 200 lb. and are tested up to 350 lb. per sq. in.

In the 5-ton wagons (1905–6), see Figs. 52 and 53, the size of engine is considerably increased, and the vertical water-tube

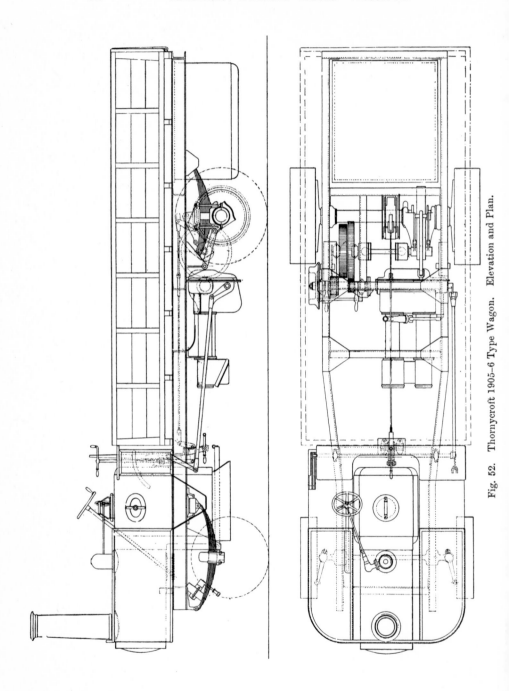

Fig. 52. Thornycroft 1905–6 Type Wagon. Elevation and Plan.

boiler is superseded by a boiler of the locomotive type (a detailed description of which will be found in the chapter on Boilers). This is an interesting departure, and will be closely watched in comparison with the water-tube boiler formerly fitted to all the

Fig. 53.   Thornycroft 1905–6 Type Wagon.

company's wagons.   For colonial use the vertical water tube will be retained.

The cylinders are 4½ in. and 7 in. in diameter respectively, the stroke being 7 in., and at normal speed of 500 revolutions per minute the engine develops 45 B.H.P.

T. COULTHARD & Co., Ltd., PRESTON

Messrs. Coulthard commenced experimenting with steam road wagons in 1895, and the author joined them in 1896, and was responsible for the various designs up to 1903. The earlier types were fitted with compound engines, uni-direction, and oil-fired boilers. Uni-direction and reversing triple-expansion engines were next fitted, but were discarded in favour of a new compound reversing pattern (patented in 1898) having two bearings, hollow piston valves, and a receiver, which also served as cover for both cylinders and piston-valve boxes. The former triple-expansion engines had also this feature in common, one cover serving for the three cylinders and piston-valve boxes. All vehicles were fitted with change-speed gears and fixed hind axle, with double side-chain transmission. 1900 saw the oil-fired boiler superseded in favour of solid fuel; and, in the last (1901) Liverpool trials this wagon was awarded a gold medal.

Fig. 54 is an external elevation of this firm's Class K 5-ton wagon, built to comply with the 1905 regulations.

	Tons	Cwt.	Qr.
The tare weight with ordinary platform is . .	4	18	2
Weight in working order	6	4	0
When loaded with 5 tons the weight, front axle =	4	4	0
„ „ „ „ hind „ =	7	10	0

The firm have long adopted the method of placing the boiler and engine between the two axles. This method has points in its favour and has since been adopted by other makers. The engine is shown in Figs. 55 and 56, and is of the compound link reversing-gear type. The cylinders are arranged with a thin wall between them so as to reduce the rocking couple to a minimum. The hollow piston valves, which are made as light as possible, are placed close to their respective cylinders to enable short direct ports to be used. Steam enters midway between the high-pressure piston-valve bearings. The exhaust from the bottom of the cylinder escapes through the piston valve, and the exhaust from the top of the cylinder through a multiplier into a receiver, which also serves as cover for both cylinders and valve boxes, one joint only being necessary. After the exhaust has passed through the receiver it enters the hollow piston valve to the bottom of the low-pressure cylinder, the top end of low-pressure cylinder being also open to the exhaust from the high-pressure. The exhaust from the top and bottom of the low-pressure cylinder is passed into the space between the working parts of the valve and thence to the silencer, which contains a feed-water heating coil. This silencer is self-contained with the engine

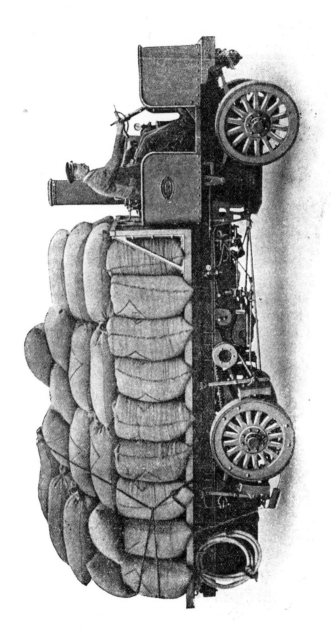

Fig. 54. Coulthard 1905–6 Type 5-Ton Wagon.

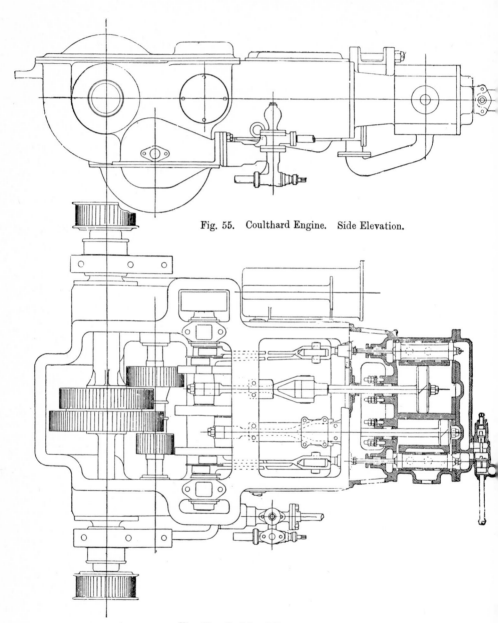

Fig. 55.   Coulthard Engine.   Side Elevation.

Fig. 56.   Coulthard Engine.   Plan.

casing. By steaming inside the
high-pressure valve, and exhaust-
ing inside the low-pressure valve,
the valve rods on the former side
must be "crossed," and on the
latter side (low-pressure) "open."

The cylinder diameters are
4 in. and 7 in. respectively, with
7 in. stroke. Normal speed, 450
revolutions per minute.

Under ordinary working conditions the exhaust from the high-
pressure cylinder has an uninterrupted flow, but when additional
power is required, the exhaust
from the high-pressure is turned
to atmosphere and live steam allowed to enter direct to the low-
pressure cylinder. The "multiplier" box is fitted with two
valves, the larger having a double
head. By moving this valve into
its second fall the smaller valve
is also lifted and shuts off communication from the high-pressure cylinder and allows steam
to enter the low-pressure cylinder
direct from the boiler.

The crank shaft carries a pinion
engaging with a spur wheel on
the second-motion shaft, which
shaft is squared in the middle.
On this square two sliding pinions
are carried (see Fig. 56), gearing
alternately with two spur rings
on the compensating gear shaft
(Fig. 57). The latter shaft is
in one piece, with one bevel
wheel bolted to the shaft and

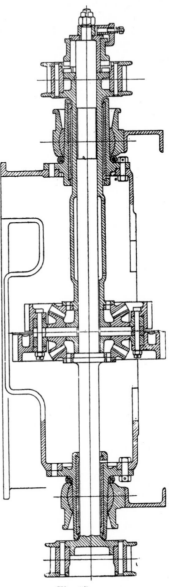

Fig. 57.

Coulthard Compensating Shaft
showing Spherical Bearings.

the other to a sleeve.   The ends of this shaft and sleeve work in spherical bearings with cushioning rings between them and the engine casing.   The cylinder end of the self-contained engine and gearing is supported by means of a universal joint.   This arrangement gives a three-point support and allows free movement in all directions, and hence no undue cross strains can be put on any working part.   From the differential shaft pinions the terminal drive is by means of two side chains on to chain rings attached to a triangular drive securely fastened to the felloes. All wheels are secured by bolts or rivets and centred.

The ram pump is worked off the second-motion shaft, and is always in gear with the engine.   It can thus be worked when the vehicle is stationary.

The boiler is illustrated in Fig. 8, and is built for a safe working pressure of 200 lb. per sq. in.   Its distinguishing feature is the absence of the usual cleaning door.   The fire bars are for this purpose hinged and can be dropped.

Steel forgings are used for the axles, which are of a rectangular section.

Gun-carriage pattern wheels are fitted, being 3 ft. in diameter, with 10½ in. face, and 2 ft. 9 in. in diameter, 6 in. face, respectively.

THE STRAKER STEAM VEHICLE Co., Ltd.

In the 1899 Liverpool trials a " Bayley" wagon fitted with the " Straker " engine and a " De Dion " boiler gave very good results from a consumptive point of view. This machine was gear driven. Then followed the " Straker" wagon, which was probably the first of the single-chain transmission type.   The boiler is a modified " De Dion " (see Fig. 11) arranged immediately over the front axle. The engine is compound, reversing and horizontal.   The rear axle is of the rotative or " live " class, the terminal chain drive being on to the differential gear.   The high-pressure is 4 in. bore and the low-pressure 7 in., with 7 in. stroke for each.   Unlike most other makers, the gear is not enclosed.   To enclose the engine and gear provides a very simple and most effective method of splash

lubrication and excludes all grit and dust.   It has been adopted by
the majority of makers, and conduces to smooth running and good
wearing of the working parts.

In the "Straker" engine the cylinder and slipper guides are
mounted on the main frame, and also the crank-shaft bearings.
On an extension of the shaft two pinions of unequal diameter are
are carried, gearing into gear wheels on the second-motion shaft
to give two speeds.   The bearings of the latter shaft are also
attached to the frame.   A sprocket pinion is fixed outside the
spur wheels on the second-motion shaft, and the drive taken by

Fig. 58.   Straker Back Axle.

a single chain of substantial strength.   Fig. 58 is an external
view of the hind axle, which is in one piece, one end of which is
attached to a driving wheel.   The other driving wheel is bolted
to a sleeve connected with the other half of the compensating
gear.

Change of speeds cannot be effected from the driver's platform.

A very simple form of locking gear is used.   This is a modification of what is found on many traction engines, and consists of
two equal-sized discs, one fitted to the differential gear and one
to a driving wheel, with a number of holes, these being so
arranged that two holes always correspond, enabling simply a pin
to be inserted through the two and thus locking the differential
gear.

The weight of the wagon is taken on two points on the back axle and one central pivot in front, so that any twisting strain to the extent of about twenty-five degrees will not affect the mechanism.

A superheater is fitted, consisting of an armoured coil round the fire box, through which the steam passes on its way to the engine and there becomes dried and superheated. This will materially assist in eliminating danger of priming.

The wheels are of the company's own type, being made entirely of mild steel other than the hubs, which are cast iron.

Fig. 59.   Straker 1905–6 Pattern Wagon.

The feed to the boiler is effected by a direct-acting, slow-speed plunger pump driven through gears off the engine crank shaft, or by means of an injector secured to the boiler.

Messrs. Straker are, in addition to building self-contained motor wagons of various capacities, constructing a light tractor suitable for hauling 4 tons of load. This is especially adapted for restrictive work where short distances are traversed and where long loading time is indispensable, as it can be employed in conjunction with several trucks or existing horse wagons. A much larger water and fuel capacity, useful as tractive weight, can be obtained, of course, than on a motor wagon. So far as the mechanism is concerned, the principles of the wagon are incorporated in the tractor.

A new model wagon (1905) has been designed to comply with the L.G.B. regulations, and this is shown in Figs. 59 and 60. The same-sized engine, hind axle, single-chain terminal drive, central pivot front axle are retained, but there are introduced several radical departures from their previous practice. A traction-engine chain type of steering is adopted, whilst a

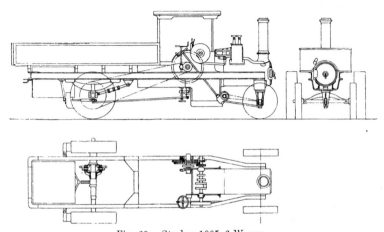

Fig. 60.   Straker 1905–6 Wagon.

locomotive type of engine, well fixed between parallel frames, makes a sound arrangement. Application of this type of boiler enables another traction-engine practice to be employed, viz. of placing the engine on the top of the boiler.

The firing is done through an ordinary fire door. The safe working pressure is 200 lb. per sq. in. The position of the engine necessitates a somewhat longer chain from the second-motion shaft, which is situated near the fire box—to the "live" axle. This chain is enclosed.

Altogether this new type is well designed, and is a good mechanical job, accessibility being its keynote.

MANN'S PATENT STEAM CART & WAGON Co., Ltd.

The first time the author had the opportunity of seeing Mann's steam cart was at the Royal Agricultural Show held at Birmingham in 1898. This machine raised a great deal of discussion owing to its departure from what was considered the right lines on which a steam road wagon should be built. It was the first application of the locomotive type of boiler to steam road wagons, and, generally, traction-engine practice was much in evidence. In the 1901 Liverpool trials (see Appendix) two of these wagons competed and did some remarkably good running. At that time a much-debated point was whether the construction of building the platform separately from the locomotive on its own wheels caused it to be classified as a separate vehicle within the meaning of the Act, or as a wagon and trailer, so that the two should not exceed 4 tons tare weight. In later models this peculiarity of construction has been abandoned, so that it is now in keeping with the general practice. The locomotive boiler is retained (it now has a greater heating surface) and the engine and transmission remain substantially the same.

Fig. 61 is a general elevation of a 5-ton standard wagon and Fig. 62 is a sectional plan.

The boiler has 48·66 sq. ft. of heating surface and 2·625 sq. ft. grate area, and has a safe working pressure of 180 lb. per sq. in. Firing is done from the side. The tare weight of this wagon is about 4 tons 18 cwt. This includes the platform, but not the detachable sides. When loaded with 5 tons the weight on the back axle is 8 tons and the weight on the front axle 3½ tons. The driving wheels are 3 ft. 6 in. in diameter with 9 in. face ; and the steering wheels 2 ft. 9 in. in diameter and 5 in. face.

In their 1905 models Messrs. Mann have somewhat modified the design, without, however, departing from the essential features of the past. The *tout ensemble* resembles less the traction engine than formerly. The locomotive-type boiler is now made much shorter and larger in diameter, and is screened in front by a fuel bunker. The engine is sunk lower between the main frame

Fig. 61.   Mann 1905–6 Type Standard Wagon.

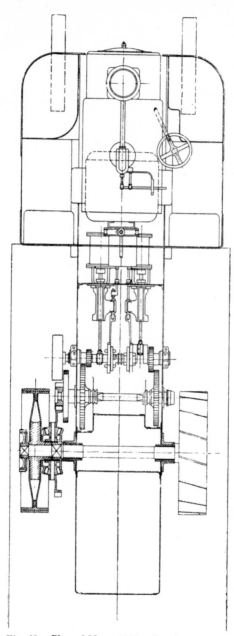

Fig. 62.   Plan of Mann 1905–6 Standard Wagon.

side plates, having sufficient head room to allow
of inspection even when
the wagon is loaded. This
arrangement allows of
the employment of a
single open-topped oil
bath for engine and gear,
these being now self-con-
tained.   The mechanism
and engine, by removal
of the top cover, can
therefore be got at in
the same way as with
the open-engine type.

The engine dimensions
are $4\frac{1}{4}$ in. high-pressure
and $6\frac{3}{4}$ in. low-pressure,
with 7 in. stroke. When
the engine is running
at 390 revolutions per
minute the road speed
is 5 miles per hour for
the fast speed, and 360
revolutions per minute
for a road speed of $2\frac{1}{2}$
miles an hour for the
slow speed.

The crank shaft is sup-
ported in two bearings
(this is as it should be),
and to the shaft are fixed
two spur pinions of un-
equal diameters alter-
nately meshing with two
spur wheels on the sec-
ond-motion shaft.   This
latter shaft is squared to
receive the wheels.   At

its end a pinion is carried which is always in gear with the spur-wheel ring on the compensating gear. One of the compensating wheels is secured to one of the road wheels, and the other to the main axle fitting on a square. In details and arrangement of parts this is a reproduction of traction-engine gearing. Steel slides are provided to guide the main axle, so that the main driving wheel shall remain in gear with the pinion on the intermediate shaft, whilst allowing proper play for the springs. These wheels do not gear on the pitch line under the varying conditions of working, though no doubt the difference is insufficient to interfere with the working, providing the teeth are of the correct length and shape.

The main frame is built of steel plates in the form of a strong box girder. These plates are extended behind the engine and carry the brackets for the intermediate gear shaft and main axle, as in traction-engine practice. The front end of the box girder supports the rear end of the boiler. All the motion work comes between the plates.

The steam valves are of the ordinary flat type, driven by the company's patent reversing gear, which has the eccentric moved by means of bell-crank levers with a distance link for keeping it parallel at all points. The gear moves the eccentrics across the crank with a straight-line motion at right angles to the crank, so that the net result so far as the valve diagrams are concerned is equivalent to that of an eccentric with varying throw working a slide valve of constant lap and constant lead.

All regulating gear is assembled close together on the foot plate, so that one man may conveniently attend to all operations. The steering gear is standardized to permit of its being fitted to either side (as the rules of the road may require in foreign countries its being placed on the left of the vehicle), the British practice being on the right.

A 2-ton wagon has lately been designed which is interesting, inasmuch as for such a weight other steam road wagon builders have displayed a tendency to employ an internal combustion engine rather than steam. The boiler is of the locomotive type. Damage to the tubes by scorching is obviated by fitting a fusible plug in the top of the fire box, which gives out before the heat can affect the tubes, in case of the water level being inadvertently allowed to get too low. The engine is single cylindered, double acting, with 4¾ in. bore and 6 in. stroke, developing 20 H.P. at its normal revolutions, viz. 550 per minute. The D slide valve is operated by the company's eccentric link motion and can be notched up to two positions either forward or reverse. The engine crank shaft carries a pinion gearing into a wheel on the second-motion shaft from which the feeding pump is operated. This shaft also carries the fast and slow main driving pinions. A drum for a powerful foot brake is also carried on the intermediate shaft. There is a double spur wheel on the back live axle with which the fast and slow pinions mesh. Smooth-faced metal to metal friction clutches are fitted on a squared portion of the intermediate shaft, and operate the fast or slow speeds without stopping the engine. The engine and second-motion shaft and gearing work in a self-contained oil bath. The same arrangement as employed on their larger wagons is adopted to keep the back axle and the intermediate shaft paralled to one another.

Messrs. FODENS, Ltd., SANDBACH, CHESHIRE

The new model (1905) is quite a new design (see Fig. 63) constructed to meet the new regulations. Traction-engine lines are as heretofore adopted; the rear live axle driven by a single chain, and other special feature of the Foden manufacture being retained. It is built to carry 5 tons on its own platform (11 ft. 6 in. by 6 ft. 6 in.), and to draw a further 2 tons on a trailer. The engine is, as in traction-engine practice, fixed on top of the boiler, rendering it very accessible, shortening steam pipes and connexions, and draining back into boiler. The steam dome acts also as a cylinder jacket, and prevents condensation of steam. The engine is compound and reversing, having a 4 in. high-pressure, and a 6½ in. low-pressure cylinder, and a stroke of 7 in., while a special type of valve is fitted by which both cylinders can —when extra power is requisite—be fed with high-pressure steam and both independently exhaust into the funnel. The boiler is of the locomotive type, constructed for 200 lb. pressure, and has a total heating surface of some 90 sq. ft., and fixed as an ordinary

Fig. 63.   Foden Wagon.

locomotive boiler, that is in front, which undoubtedly takes up an unusual length of non-carrying space. Roughly speaking, the boiler is fixed between two channels, which makes a good mechanical job.

A two-speed gear (giving at normal revolutions of engine speeds of 3 and 6 miles an hour) is arranged. The power is transmitted from the second-motion shaft by a large " Renold " chain passing to the differential on the driving axle. The rear wheels are 3 ft. 6 in. in diameter by 10 in. face, and the front wheels 2 ft. 9 in. by 5 in. face. The front of the machine is supported by a transverse spring and a steering turn-table. The water tank holds 170 gallons.

THE YORKSHIRE PATENT STEAM WAGON Co., LEEDS

The vehicles built by this company strike out on original lines and possess many novel features.

Fig. 64 is an external view of a 5-ton machine designed to meet the requirements of the 1905 Board of Trade regulations. The boiler is of the fire-tube type, and is placed, unlike all other makers', transversely and immediately over the front axle. It has 53·3 sq. ft. of heating surface and 2·65 of grate area (see Fig. 12), and constructed for a working pressure of 200 lb. per sq. in. The products of combustion are divided and drawn equally through the tubes running in opposite directions and returning to a common smoke box. The fire door is arranged above the foot plate.

The engine is of the compound type and fixed on the outside of the frame. The high-pressure cylinder has a bore of $4\frac{1}{2}$ in., and the low-pressure cylinder $7\frac{1}{2}$ in., both having a $7\frac{1}{2}$ in. stroke. The engine runs at 450 revolutions per minute. Single eccentric reversing gear is used, operated by a sliding boss on the crank shaft, in the movement of which the eccentric is thrown backward or forward as required. It can be notched up in the usual way as with the ordinary link motion. The valves are of the flat type, with the chests on the sides of the cylinders.

Fig. 64. Yorkshire Co.'s 1905–6 Wagon.

Fig. 65 shows the method of transmission of power to the driving wheels. The crank shaft is carried in two inverted pedestals bolted to the main frame; to each of these pedestals a steel bracket is hinged, which carries the second-motion shaft and driving-axle bearings. The outer ends of these brackets are free to slide on strong guides. Laminated springs, fixed to the brackets by joint pins, carry the main frame, which can rise and fall without any material variation in the working centres of the shafts. There are only two bearings to each shaft, and all the gearing is between them. The second-motion shaft and the driving axle run in swivel bearings, so that, on uneven roads, the shafts cannot bind in the necks. The differential gear is attached to the driving axle and sleeve, the latter being secured to one wheel and the

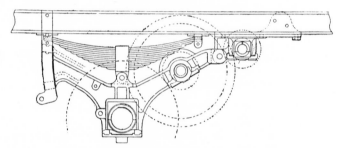

Fig. 65.   Yorkshire Co.'s Method of Transmission.

main axle to the other.   Drag rods are fitted to relieve the strain on the spokes of the driving wheels.   A large spur wheel is fixed on the compensating gear centre, which is always in gear with the pinion on second-motion shaft, and the variation of speed is effected by the use of a double sliding pinion on a square, gearing into fast and slow speed wheels keyed on to the second-motion shaft and operated from the driver's seat. The speeds provided are $2\frac{1}{2}$ and 5 miles an hour, with the engine running at 450 revolutions per minute—its normal speed.

The whole of the gearing in the latest pattern is contained in a dust-proof and oil-retaining casing, which is a step in the right direction. The older makers, some time ago, found the necessity for this, and buyers attach importance to this essential protection.

	Tons.	Cwt.	Qr.
5-*ton size*—Tare weight	4	15	0
Light—Weight on front axle	2	0	0
Weight on hind axle	2	15	0
Loaded with 5 tons—Weight on front axle . .	3	10	0
Weight on hind axle . .	7	5	0

The steering is on the Ackerman system. The brakes are the ordinary single-shoe pattern. A boiler feed pump is worked by reduction from the crank shaft, and can be run when the vehicle is stationary.

Gun-carriage wheels are usually supplied.

THE " LONDONDERRY " STEAM WAGON
(SEAHAM HARBOUR)

Lord Londonderry's Seaham Harbour Engine Works have more recently taken up the construction of steam wagons. Having always a large staff of emergency men to keep for repair work for colliery wagons, locomotives, etc., steam wagons were originally decided upon to keep these men in constant work, but now that the wagons have been in use some time, with pronounced success, this branch is receiving its full support. The latest type (see Fig. 66) fulfils the 1905 regulations, and has 3 ft. 3 in. driving wheels with 10 in. tyres, and 2 ft. 9 in. front wheels with 6 in. tyres. Cast-steel wheels (with no rivets or joints) or the company's composite wheel are fitted. The drive is taken to the driving-wheel peripheries by extended arms on naves. Cast-steel side frames carry crank and second-motion shaft. Slots are machined in the side frames with radius from centre of second shaft, and perfect meshing and alignment are secured under all circumstances by the axle boxes sliding in the said slots. Under very trying experiments this method has been found to act very well.

The boiler is of the central-fired vertical fire-tube type, with 200 lb. working pressure, with hand holes and mud-hole doors to facilitate cleaning of the fire box, etc. The shell, of very strong construction, contains fire box and central feeding tube. Attached

Fig. 66.   Londonderry 5-Ton Wagon.

to the central tube is the top tube plate, the fire tubes (weldless steel) being expanded in the furnace crown and tube plate. Four large cleaning doors are provided, enabling fire-box sides and tube plate to be cleaned. Wash-out and mud-hole doors are provided at top and bottom of shell. A boiler of this type is claimed by the makers to have been in constant use in their own works for fourteen years, with little cost for repairs. This is apparently for stationary work, and is no criterion that for vehicle work it will be so satisfactory.

Firing is done from the top through a central chute, and the fire bars and ash pan can be raised or lowered at driver's will. The boiler mountings are in gun metal, and can all be cleaned whilst full pressure of steam is on boiler. To sweep external of tubes the chimney can be detached, exposing the whole length of tubes. Feed water is supplied by an automatic feed pump (geared down from the engine crank shaft), which can be thrown out of gear for pumping when vehicle is standing. An injector is fitted to feed independently when required. The boiler is placed with all handles and control capable of being worked ordinarily by one man.

The engine is a horizontal compound, fitted with a loco-type flat valve. The valve motion is the firm's patent single eccentric with constant lead and variable cut-off. The dimensions of cylinders are $4\frac{1}{4}$ in. and 7 in., by 7 in. stroke respectively. Large working surfaces are provided throughout, and the engine is enclosed in an oil-tight, dust-proof casing. Both cylinders may for emergencies be worked as high-pressure.

To obtain smooth and quiet running all gearing (steel) is machine cut. Crank-shaft pinions slide on squared portion of shaft, driving gear wheels on a second-motion shaft. A positive feed-pump lubricator supplies oil to the slide valves and cylinders, the splash principle being employed for the engine crank, etc. Grease lubricators are used on axles and shafts.

The speeds provided are $5\frac{1}{2}$ and $2\frac{1}{2}$ miles per hour. Water capacity, 220 gallons, equal to 26 miles' running; coke, 4 cwt., equal to 35 to 40 miles.

The main axle is of 5 in. diameter. A live fore axle gives the vehicle a three-point suspension to obviate twists on frame.

One of the features of the "Londonderry" is the suspension of the front axle, which is carried by ordinary semi-elliptic springs from a separate under frame, thereby forming a " bogie carriage," which is pivoted, so that any twisting strain, caused by one wheel being raised only, cannot be transmitted to any part of the vehicle.

JAMES ROBERTSON & SON, FLEETWOOD

This firm's 5-ton wagon is illustrated in Fig. 67.

The engine is of the compound link reversing type, having 4 in. high-pressure cylinder and 7 in. low-pressure cylinder, both having a stroke of 5 in., and running normally at 425 revolutions per minute, developing 25 B.H.P. A " live " steam arrangement is fitted to the low-pressure cylinder. Lubrication is effected by the splash method, oil being carried in an enclosed crank case.

Outside the engine casing the crank shaft is square, and on this slides a double pinion of unequal diameter, gearing alternately with spur wheels on the differential gear shaft, which carries at its end chain pinions, the terminal drive being taken by roller chains attached to chain rings on the driving wheels. The differential gear may, at will, be locked. The gear ratios are 10 and 17·8 to 1.

The boiler (see Fig. 13) is of the horizontal fire-tube variety, centrally fired. The grate area is 2½ sq. ft. and the heating surface 82 sq. ft. Working pressure, 200 lb. per sq. in. The fire bars, with the ash pan, are slung into position by steel ropes, and are raised or lowered as required for cleaning or lighting purposes by suitable worm gearing.

The main boiler feed pump is worked off the engine by reduced gearing. The water heater is of the marine type, having a filter of cloth or coke, and being fixed well above the tank level. All condensed steam passes to the tank. This is a good arrangement, and might advantageously be employed on all wagons, as it conduces to economy of water and overcomes the constant dripping from the ash pan, where the condensed steam is usually allowed to run.

The wheels generally are of the gun-carriage type, with a

diameter of 3 ft. 3 in. for the driving wheels and $10\frac{1}{2}$ in. face, and the front wheels 2 ft. 9 in. diameter and 6 in. face.

The steering is on the Ackerman principle, actuated by means of a vertical screw having double square threads engaging on a steel case-hardened wheel on the shaft.

The front axle works in horn plates, the weight being taken in the centre by an inverted laminated spring with the points bearing at the outer ends of the axle. By securing the axle in the centre a three-point support is assured.

Fig. 67. Robertson 5-Ton Wagon.

The wagon is designed to comply with the 1905 regulations, and will carry 5 tons and 2 tons on a trailer. The principal dimensions are: length, 16 ft. 9 in.; width, 6 ft. 5 in.; wheel base, 9 ft.; tread centre of tyres, 5 ft. $10\frac{1}{4}$ in.; height of platform when light, 4 ft.; platform, 13 ft. 4 in. by 6 ft. 5 in.

In their tipping wagons Messrs. Robertson have introduced hydraulic power.

GARRETT & SONS, LEICESTER

The vehicle embodies several unusual features, although in appearance it conforms with the ordinary type of lorry (see Fig. 68). The engine is compound but non-reversing, the link motion being therefore dispensed with, and the reverse provided by sliding spur wheels. The benefit of this departure from common practice is not apparent. It is conceivable that where a motive power is in itself incapable of being reversed, as in an explosion engine, additional gearing as now required would not be resorted to as if this were otherwise, but rather that the power itself be directed in the opposite direction. Several steam wagons were in the early stages fitted with a non-reversing engine, but the practice has since been abandoned. The reversing of a steam engine may also be used as a very powerful brake, although this feature cannot be urged against the type under review, as a special controlling valve by which the cylinders may be made both high-pressure can also be made to close the exhaust from the high-pressure cylinder in order to use the engine as a brake. At the same time that the high-pressure steam is admitted to the low-pressure cylinder a port is opened to pass the steam direct to the exhaust pipe from the high-pressure cylinder. By this means the benefit of increased high-pressure area is obtained, and this is not merely the difference between the respective areas of the two cylinders, as is the case on many other vehicles.

The boiler is of the vertical fire-tube class, top fired, the exhaust steam being passed through a drier previous to ejection through funnel. The engine and gearing are self-contained in one casing, and carried from the frame on a three-point suspension. The wheels are all cast steel. Foot pedals operate internal hub brakes, and the usual tyre brakes are also fitted.

Fig. 68.   Garrett Wagon.

Fig. 69.   Single-Screw Tipping Gear.

TIP WAGONS

TIP WAGONS are largely used by contractors, municipal authorities, colliery proprietors, etc., and the different manufacturers have their own designs. As the majority of these are similar in principle, it is only necessary to describe an example, which includes the majority of makers, and one or two recent departures. The usual type is known as the "end tipper." For special purposes, however, end tipping is not feasible, and "side tippers" may be substituted. When possible, however, the latter should be avoided owing to the extra height required, which interferes with the loading. Nothing like so good a mechanical application can be obtained as in the "end tipper."

In Fig. 69 is shown a tipping arrangement designed by the author some years ago, and similar arrangements are employed by quite a large number of makers. A single screw is used for raising and lowering the body, and can be operated by handles from either side of the wagon. Some makers use two screws, but, providing the design is good, one is really all that is necessary.

Fig. 70.   Telescopic-Screw Tipping Gear.

109

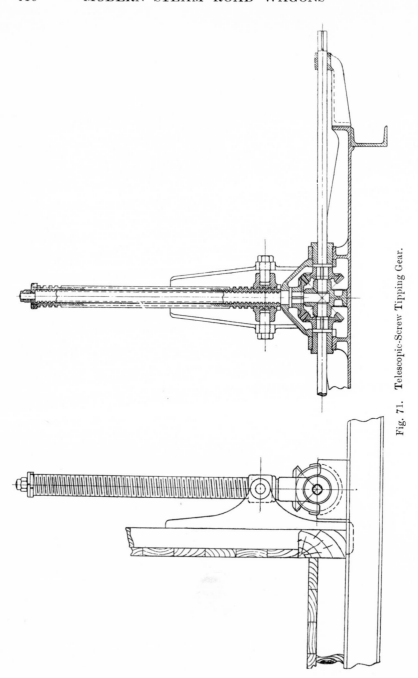

Fig. 71. Telescopic-Screw Tipping Gear.

Fig. 72.   Telescopic-Screw Tipping Gear.   Operated by Engine.

Latterly the Lancashire Steam Motor Co. have fitted an improved end-tipping device, the distinguishing feature of which is a telescopic screw, and the arrangement is shown in Figs. 70 and 71. The inner screw is of a finer pitch than the outer. Motion is given to the screw by bevel wheels operated by side handles, or the same can be coupled up and worked by the engine. The first half of the lift required is done by the inner screw, and, being of a fine pitch, at a comparatively slow speed. When, however, the top of the inner screw is reached the outer one commences to revolve, and, being of coarser pitch, the speed of the lifting is accelerated as the work, due to the angle of the body, is

Fig. 73.   Robertson's Hydraulic Tipping Gear.

decreased. By this means a very short and strong screw is obtained.

Fig. 72 shows a mechanically operated tipping gear made by the same firm.

The telescopic screw as described is the same, but the motion is given to the screw by means of friction cones on the engine shaft, bevel wheels transmitting the power to the cross shaft through a worm and worm wheel. Any possible damage which might be occasioned by overwinding is provided against, as the outer screw has at its extreme end a collar which, when the screw is fully extended, offers sufficient resistance to cause the clutches

Fig. 74. Mann's Tipping Gear.

I

to slip. The same thing occurs when the engine is reversed and
the body is brought down to its lowest position.

Robertson's hydraulic gear is shown in Fig. 73. This consists
of a hydraulic cylinder, the ram of which is connected to the
under side of the body. The raising of the ram is preferably
done by means of a small auxiliary steam pump, the return
water escaping to the water tank, but the ram may also be
raised by the main boiler feeding pump. There is no reason why
the ram should not be raised by connecting the under side of
ram to the waterleg of the boiler.

The screws commonly employed are by Messrs. Mann's Patent

Fig. 75. Straker's Side-Tipping Gear.

Steam Cart and Wagon Co. replaced by racks made of a mild
steel plate and pins into which a gear wheel engages. This is
clearly shown in the illustration of their tipping wagon in
Fig. 74. The gear wheel fits on a square shaft which, in turn, is
rotated by means of a worm and wheel from the driver's foot-
plate. It is completely non-reversible through the use of the
worm, and is therefore as safe as a screw gear, and one man can
tip the load easily and quickly. The construction of the racks
makes it impossible for the gear to get blocked up, however thickly
coated it may become with mud, and its efficiency is practically
unaffected by dirt.

A "side-tipping" wagon as built by Messrs. Straker & Co. is

illustrated in Fig. 75. It will be observed that to enable the side-tipping gear to be arranged so that the tipping centre shall be on the centre line of the wagon it is necessary to raise the body to a great height. This is unavoidable and discounts " side tippers," which are only in use where end tippers are not applicable.

LUBRICATION

THE efficient lubrication of motor wagons is of paramount importance, and that such a small amount of attention has hitherto been given to it is remarkable.

When it is remembered that every detail in the construction of such vehicles receives, in most cases, exact scientific treatment, and that all the materials are carefully selected, the stresses accurately ascertained and allowed for, and the working parts proportioned so as to give the highest efficiency, and yet all the labour thus entailed may be negatived by insufficient and unscientific lubrication, either as regards the method of application or in the selection of the lubricants themselves, it will be evident that lubrication ought not be relegated to the rank of a secondary consideration, but the subject should claim our very serious and unremitting investigation in order to obtain the best possible results. Those who have made a careful study of the subject, know that the lack of attention to lubrication is responsible for many of the unsatisfactory results, unreliable working, and breakdowns.

Locomotive engineers have fully realized the importance of this subject, and it has received almost equal consideration as the design of the engine itself. The result is that the best methods of applying the lubricants are adopted, and extreme care is exercised in the selection of the lubricants themselves. In fact, lubrication is brought to a high degree of perfection, the consumption of oil per mile is given with certainty, and, if the amount is exceeded, explanations are required from those in charge.

When a contrast is made between the working conditions of the locomotive with its prepared track, made practically level and smooth, and the motor road wagon which has to take the roads as they come, rough and smooth, with heavy gradients and constantly varying loads, the working conditions of the latter are far more exacting, and the question of lubrication deserves more than the cursory attention it has generally received hitherto.

Necessity is, however, now causing manufacturers to look more carefully into the question than they were formerly wont to do, and before long, no doubt, the present methods will be improved upon, and the same state of perfection will be attained as appertains on railways.

Lubrication may be divided into two sections, viz. (1) Cylinder and (2) Engine lubrication, each requiring separate and entirely different treatment.

CYLINDER LUBRICATION.—The pistons and valves are usually lubricated by means of ordinary drench cups of various designs. These are so familiar as to require no special description.

The fault of these lies in the fact that they are not automatic, and everything is left to the discretion of the driver as to how often they should be filled. Usually there is nothing to indicate whether the lubricator is full or empty without a personal examination. This, of course, is highly objectionable when negotiating street traffic in daylight, but especially so in the night time.

Again, the lubricator may be filled with lubricant, and yet, owing to the passages being blocked up, the lubricant may not reach the valves or pistons. How many broken parts have been occasioned by such a cause, but usually attributed to bad design or material, which, had the lubrication been right, would not have occurred.

Another objection attending this form of lubricator is that directly it is refilled it may or it may not pass at once into the valve chest and be emptied immediately. There is no certainty or real provision to guard against the former contingency anyhow.

For the efficient lubrication of valves and pistons the oil must be fed regularly drop by drop. There are several types of lubricators to effect this now in use, known as (1) mechanically driven or pump lubricators and (2) steam driven or displacement lubricators.

The former are generally considered to be the more positive, but they are undoubtedly complicated and require to be driven from some part of the engine, and they are also very liable to become deranged and so become useless, or, rather, worse than useless, a positive danger.

In the steam-driven or displacement type there are two classes, the commoner form being composed simply of an oil reservoir with the necessary pipe connexions and sight feed glass, the reservoir being connected to the boiler by means of a steam pipe having a condenser in the shape of a coil or cylinder fitted thereto. A head of water is in this way afforded which displaces the oil and forces it into the steam chest.

Although this type of lubricator possesses great advantages over the drench cup and pump forms, it is far from being perfect under all conditions of working. If the road be very rough and there is an abundance of ruts the lurching of the wagon causes the lubricator to work spasmodically, owing to the varying head of water. To militate against this it is better to charge it with glycerine, the difference between its specific gravity and water enabling the drop of oil to pass out of the centre.

Again, this type has a tendency when the vehicle is running down a gradient with steam valve closed to race and syphon the oil out of the reservoir too rapidly or altogether. This may likewise occur when the wagon is standing, due to the formation of a vacuum in the pipes.

Fig. 76. "Wakefield" Automatic Lubricator.

A lubricator which the author has extensively used (the "Wakefield," Fig. 76) certainly overcomes all the defects before enumerated and can be recommended. It is a special form of steam-driven lubricator, and is now being widely adopted. It does not rely on condensation at all. The construction is simple, the steam being taken direct into the oil reservoir, and after the oil has passed through the sight feed glass it is met by a jet of steam on the injector principle, which drives it forward into the steam chest. It also has the effect of atomizing the oil, giving more perfect lubrication, for when in this condition it is more readily diffused over the parts to be lubricated.

When once set the feed is always regular, irrespective of the road and engine conditions, and the oil cannot syphon.

The lubricator ought to be fitted in front of the driver, and the method of operation should be as follows. The sight feed glass must be filled with glycerine in preference to water, as, owing to its greater viscosity, the oil does not reach the side of the glass, which thus always remains perfectly clean. The usual regulating valve for steam admission, and the valve for regulating the supply of oil, etc., are denoted in the figure.

The arrangement of an auxiliary bye-pass to feed should the sight feed glass be accidentally broken is decidedly a good idea, and enables the lubricator always to keep working, except when it is empty or when steam is shut off from it.

Lubricant.—The selection of the right class of lubricant is by no means a simple problem, as there are so many varieties from which to select. Experience has shown that the best results are obtained from the black hydrocarbon cylinder oils, and not the light variety.

Of the black hydrocarbon oils there are unlimited varieties at all prices, and it ought to be mentioned at the outset that the price per gallon ought to be entirely disregarded, as it is no criterion of the quality or suitability to the work. The cost per mile should in all cases be the method of comparing lubricants which are satisfactory from every other point of view, but vary in price per gallon.

For wagons using ordinary saturated steam the best results are obtainable by using an oil which is compounded; but for wagons using superheated steam an absolutely pure hydrocarbon oil is essential.

The steam pressure generally adopted by motor-wagon manufacturers is 200 lb. per sq. in., and for this pressure the oil ought to have a fire test of 600 degrees.

For superheated steam the fire test ought to be 700 to 800 degrees.

The cost per mile will, of course, depend entirely on circumstances, but an all-round figure would be 0·03 pence; or, put in quantity, say 1 pint for every 35 miles.

The author has recently interested himself in exhaustive experiments with graphite as a substitute for oil for cylinder lubrication. This has been used by itself, and also mixed with oil in varying proportions. The results, however, have been the same in both cases; it does very well at first, but it requires a great deal of attention; is, moreover, very costly, and seems to have a tendency to slowly fill up the ports and reduce the lead of the valves. Small balls of graphite have also been taken from the cylinders resembling small birds' eggs after a few weeks' use. Owing to the wide difference in specific gravity it is a difficult matter to successfully mix graphite with oil. It is, however, very useful where a cylinder has been badly scored, as it fills up the erosions and prevents further damage.

ENGINE LUBRICATION.—There are three systems of engine lubrication: (1) drop or gravity, by means of oil cups and boxes; (2) splash lubrication; and (3) forced lubrication.

The first-named system was the one generally in vogue a few years ago. Later, the lubricant was applied by means of small oilers, or in some cases boxes, having syphons fixed to them and pipes leading to the various bearings. This latter method, however, proved very wasteful and inefficient; in fact, there was too much "hit and miss" about it (oftener miss than hit), with a consequent loss of lubricant, etc.

The splash system has now almost entirely superseded the drop or gravity system. In this case the whole of the engine (and often the gearing) is enclosed in a suitable oil-tight case, the lubricant being directly in contact with the working parts and splashed about by the cranks, etc. The whole of the working parts are thus practically working in an oil bath.

This method is at once economical and efficient, as when the engine-case is once filled with a suitable oil it will run for several months without being changed, all that is required being a small addition of oil from time to time to make up for unavoidable losses, due mainly to leakage. Thus any damage that might accrue to working parts by derangements of oil-feeding mechanism, stoppage of pipes, etc., is effectually surmounted.

Very great care ought to be exercised in the selection of the lubricant used. What is required is an oil which will not thicken or have any tendency to sludge, due to gland leakages allowing condensed water containing cylinder oil to find its way into the crank chamber.

It will also be evident that if the wrong kind of lubricant is employed, that the fact of the churning up which it is constantly receiving causes a great internal resistance, resulting, of course, in a low efficiency.

There are many so-called "suitable" oils on the market which are supplied for motor-wagon lubrication, but which are, in reality, most unsuitable, as they act as an internal brake, and the efficiency of the motor is reduced at the same time that the fuel consumption is increased.

An absolutely pure hydrocarbon oil is a *sine qua non ;* and any oil having the slightest trace of animal, fish, or vegetable element in its composition should be strictly avoided, as these oils with a slight admixture of water saponify and make an emulsion.

Forced lubrication, which has proved itself an unqualified success in high-speed engines of larger sizes, has not yet been tried to any great extent in connexion with motor wagons, and it is doubtful, owing to the small size of engine employed, whether the complications of extra oil pipes and connexions would not negative any advantages to be derived from this system.

THE NEW REGULATIONS

THE following is the text of the New Order controlling heavy motor cars exceeding two tons in weight unladen, and any trailer drawn by a heavy motor car.

"ARTICLE I.—*Commencement of Regulations.*—The Regulations in this Order (herein-after referred to as 'the Regulations') shall come into operation on the first day of March, one thousand nine hundred and five, and that date is herein-after referred to as the commencement of the Regulations.

"ARTICLE II.—*Definitions.*—In the Regulations—

"*Heavy Motor Car.*—The expression 'heavy motor car' means a motor car exceeding two tons in weight unladen.

"*Trailer.*—The expression 'trailer' means a vehicle drawn by a heavy motor car.

"*Registering Authority.*—The expression 'registering authority' means, in relation to a heavy motor car, the Council of a County, or the Council of a County Borough, by whom the heavy motor car has been, or can be, registered, in pursuance of the Motor Car Act, 1903, and of the Motor Car (Registration and Licensing) Order, 1903.

"*Axle-weight.*—The expression 'axle-weight' means, in relation to an axle of a heavy motor car, or of a trailer, the aggregate weight transmitted to the surface of the road or other base whereon the heavy motor car or the trailer moves or rests, by the several wheels attached to that axle when the heavy motor car, or the trailer, is loaded.

"*Registered Axle-weight.*—The expression 'registered axle-weight' means, in relation to an axle of a heavy motor car, the axle-weight of that axle, as registered by the registering authority in pursuance of the Regulations.

"*Width.*—The expression 'width,' in relation to the tire of a wheel, means the distance measured horizontally and in a straight line across the circumference of the wheel and between the two points in the outer surface of the tire which are farthest apart.

"*Diameter.*—The expression 'diameter,' in relation to a wheel, means the diameter measured between the two opposite points in the outer surface of the tire which are farthest apart.

"*Weight.*—The expression 'weight,' in relation to a heavy motor car or trailer, when unladen, means the weight of the vehicle exclusive of the weight of any water, fuel, or accumulators used for the purpose of propulsion.

"ARTICLE III.—*Increase of weights, unladen.*—Notwithstanding anything in the Motor Car Acts, 1896 and 1903, and except as is otherwise provided in the Regulations, a heavy motor car may be used on a highway if the weight of the heavy motor car unladen does not exceed five tons, or if the weight of the heavy motor car unladen with the weight of an unladen vehicle drawn by it does not exceed six and a half tons.

"ARTICLE IV.—*Registration of Weights.*—(1) On every application to a registering authority for the registration of a heavy motor car, the owner shall declare—

"(*a*) The weight of the heavy motor car unladen.

"(*b*) The axle-weight of each axle ; and

"(*c*) The diameter of each wheel.

"(2)—(*a*) Before a heavy motor car is registered, the weight of the car unladen, and, if the registering authority so direct, the axle-weight of each axle of the car, shall be ascertained by or in the presence of an officer of the registering authority. That officer shall certify the weight or weights so ascertained, and shall make any necessary correction in the statement of weights declared by the owner.

"(*b*) The officer of the registering authority shall also satisfy himself that the tires of the wheels of the car, if the tires are not pneumatic, or are not made of a soft or elastic material, are of the dimensions required by the Regulations.

"(*c*) The owner of a heavy motor car shall, for the purpose of this condition, cause the motor car to be driven or brought to any such place as the registering authority appoint.

"(3) Upon the registration of a heavy motor car,—

"(*a*) the weight of the heavy motor car unladen, as certified as aforesaid,

"(*b*) the axle-weight of each axle,

"(*c*) the diameter of each wheel,

"(*d*) the width and material of the tire of each wheel, and

"(*e*) the highest rate of speed at which, in conformity with the Regulations, the heavy motor car may be driven without a trailer, shall be entered in the Register of Motor Cars.

"(4) Upon receiving from the registering authority a copy of the entries made in the register relating to a heavy motor car, the owner of the heavy motor car shall cause—

"(i) the registered weight of the heavy motor car unladen,

"(ii) the registered axle-weight of each axle, and

"(iii) the highest rate of speed at which, in conformity with the Regulations, the heavy motor car may be driven without a trailer, to be painted, or otherwise plainly marked, in the first and second case, upon some conspicuous part of the right or off side of the heavy motor car, and, in the third case, upon some conspicuous part of the left or near side of the heavy motor car.

"The owner of the heavy motor car shall cause the aforesaid particulars to be painted or marked in letters and figures not less than one inch in height, and of such shape and colour as to be clearly legible and clearly distinguishable from the colour of the ground whereon the letters and figures are painted or marked: and he shall cause all the paint or marking to be from time to time repaired or renewed, as often as may be necessary to keep the said letters and figures clearly legible and clearly distinguishable.

"(5) The owner of a heavy motor car which has been registered before, and which is in use at, the commencement of the Regulations, shall, within six months thereafter, either cause the heavy motor car to be registered anew, or shall cause the heavy motor car to be brought before an officer of the registering authority with whom the heavy motor car has been already registered.

"In either case the procedure prescribed by this Article shall be followed with respect to the heavy motor car, as if it were a heavy motor car the owner whereof is for the first time an applicant for registration; but in the latter case no registration fee shall be charged by the registering authority in respect of the heavy motor car, or in respect of the procedure prescribed by this Article; and in the case of a heavy motor car the weight of which, when unladen, exceeds five tons but does not exceed seven tons, and which has been registered before the first day of September, one thousand nine hundred and four, compliance with the procedure prescribed by this Article shall, notwithstanding any other provision of the Regulations, have effect as a sufficient authority for the use of the heavy motor car on a highway.

" The registering authority shall furnish the owner of a heavy motor car with a certificate in an appropriate form, to the effect that the procedure prescribed by this Article has been followed, and that the heavy motor car may be used on a highway without further registration.

" On the expiration of six months from the commencement of the Regulations, a heavy motor car which has been registered before the commencement of the Regulations, and in respect of which the procedure prescribed by this Article has not been followed shall not, except for the purpose of being registered, be used on any highway until the heavy motor car has been registered anew; and all previous registration of the heavy motor car shall cease to have effect.

"(6) Nothing in the Regulations shall have effect so as to require the registering authority to register a heavy motor car which does not in all particulars satisfy each condition rendered applicable by the Regulations to the heavy motor car or in respect of which there has been a failure to comply with the procedure prescribed by this Article.

" ARTICLE V.—*Axle-weights.*—(1) The axle-weight of an axle of a heavy motor car shall not exceed the registered axle-weight.

"(2) The registered axle-weight of an axle of a heavy motor car shall not exceed eight tons, and the sum of the registered axle-weights of all the axles of a heavy motor car shall not exceed twelve tons.

" ARTICLE VI.—*Tires.*—(1) The tire of each wheel of a heavy motor car shall be smooth, and shall, where the tire touches the surface of the road or other base whereon the heavy motor car moves or rests, be flat :

" Provided that the edges of the tire may be bevelled or rounded to the extent in the case of each edge of not more than half an inch :

" Provided also that, if the tire is constructed of separate plates, the plates may be separated by parallel spaces which shall be disposed throughout the outer surface of the tire so that nowhere shall the aggregate extent of the space or spaces in the course of a straight line drawn horizontally across the circumference of the wheel exceed one-eighth part of the width of the tire.

" (2) The width of the tire of each wheel of a heavy motor car shall be determined by such of the following conditions as may apply to the circumstances of the case ; that is to say,—

" (a) The width shall in every case be not less than five inches.

" (b) The width shall be not less than that number of half inches which is equal to the number of units of registered axle-weight of the axle to which the wheel is attached.

" The unit of registered axle-weight shall vary according to the diameter of the wheel, and the rules set forth in the subjoined scale ; that is to say,—

" (i) If the wheel is three feet in diameter, the unit of registered axle-weight shall be seven and a half hundredweights ;

" (ii) If the wheel exceeds three feet in diameter, the unit of registered axle-weight shall be seven and a half hundredweights, with an addition of weight in the proportion of one hundredweight for every twelve inches by which the diameter is increased beyond three feet ; and in the same proportion for any increase which is greater or less than twelve inches ; and

" (iii) If the wheel is less than three feet in diameter, the unit of registered axle-weight shall be seven and a half hundredweights, with a deduction of weight in the proportion of one hundredweight for every six inches by which the diameter is reduced below three feet ; and in the same proportion for any reduction which is greater or less than six inches.

" (3) This Article shall not apply to any tire which is pneumatic or which is made of a soft or elastic material.

" ARTICLE VII.—*Speed.*—The speed at which a heavy motor car is driven on any highway shall not exceed eight miles an hour :

" Provided that—

" (*a*) If the weight of the heavy motor car unladen exceeds three tons ; or

" (*b*) If the registered axle-weight of any axle exceeds six tons ; or

" (*c*) If the heavy motor car draws a trailer, the speed shall not exceed five miles an hour.

" Provided also that—

" If the heavy motor car has all its wheels fitted with pneumatic tires or with tires made of a soft or elastic material, the speed at which the heavy motor car may be driven on any highway shall not exceed—

" (*a*) Twelve miles an hour—Where the registered axle-weight of any axle does not exceed six tons ; and

" (*b*) Eight miles an hour—Where the registered axle-weight of any axle exceeds six tons.

" ARTICLE VIII.—*Size of Wheels.*—The diameter of a wheel of a heavy motor car, if the wheel is fitted with a tire which is not pneumatic or is not made of a soft or elastic material, shall be not less than two feet.

" ARTICLE IX.—*Width.*—Notwithstanding anything in the Motor Cars (Use and Construction) Order, 1904, a heavy motor car, if its weight unladen is three tons or exceeds three tons, and any trailer drawn by any such heavy motor car may, when measured between its extreme projecting points, be of a width not exceeding seven feet six inches.

" ARTICLE X.—*Springs.*—Every heavy motor car shall be constructed with suitable and sufficient springs between each axle and the frame of the heavy motor car.

" ARTICLE XI.—*Trailers.*—(1) The owner of a trailer shall cause to be painted, or otherwise plainly marked, upon some conspicuous part of the right or off' side of the trailer, in letters and figures not less than one inch in height, and of such shape and colour as to be clearly legible and clearly distinguishable from the colour of the ground whereon the letters and figures are painted or marked,—

" (*a*) The weight of the trailer unladen ; and

"(b) The axle-weight of each axle of the trailer, if the weight of the trailer unladen exceeds one ton.

"He shall cause the paint or marking to be from time to time repaired or renewed, as often as may be necessary to keep the said letters and figures clearly legible and clearly distinguishable.

"(2) The Regulations so far as they relate to the width of the tires and the size of the wheels of a heavy motor car, the wheels whereof are fitted with tires which are not pneumatic or are not made of a soft or elastic material, shall, with the necessary modifications, apply and have effect with respect to a trailer exceeding one ton in weight unladen, with the substitution in the Regulations of three inches for five inches as the minimum width of the tires, and of references to the axle-weights painted or marked upon the trailer in pursuance of this Article for references to registered axle-weights.

"(3) The axle-weight of an axle of a trailer shall not exceed four tons.

"(4) Every trailer shall be constructed with suitable and sufficient springs between each axle and the frame of the trailer.

"(5) A heavy motor car which is used either as a stage carriage or otherwise for the conveyance of passengers for gain or hire, shall not draw a trailer.

"ARTICLE XII.—*Ascertainment of Weights by Officers of Councils.*—If a heavy motor car is upon a highway within a distance not exceeding half a mile by road from a public weighing machine, or other weighing machine which is conveniently accessible, and which belongs to or is subject to the control, or may be used for any purposes of a registering authority or of any other Council having control of the highway, and a duly authorised officer of the registering authority or other Council has reasonable ground for ascertaining whether the axle-weight for the time being of any axle of the heavy motor car, or of the trailer drawn by the heavy motor car exceeds the registered or marked axle-weight of that axle, the officer may require the person driving or in charge of the heavy motor car to drive the heavy motor car with or without the trailer, or to cause the heavy motor car to be driven with or without the trailer to the weighing machine, and the said officer may then cause the axle-weight for the time being of any axle to be ascertained; and the person driving or in charge of the heavy motor car shall comply with any such requirement, and shall, to the best of his ability, afford all such facilities as may be reasonably necessary for the purpose of ascertaining the axle-weight as aforesaid.

"ARTICLE XIII.—*Breach of Regulations. Saving for Existing Heavy Motor Cars.*—No person shall cause or permit to be used on any highway, or shall on any highway drive or have charge of, a heavy motor car or a trailer which is not in all respects in accordance with the Regulations so far as they relate to the use and construction of heavy motor cars or trailers, as the case may be, or which is so used or driven as to contravene the Regulations :

"Provided that during a period of six months after the commencement of the Regulations any failure to comply with the Regulations so far as they relate to the use or construction of heavy motor cars or trailers shall not be deemed to be a breach or contravention of the Regulations, if the failure occurs solely in relation to a heavy motor car registered before, or to a trailer which is in use at, the commencement of the Regulations.

"ARTICLE XIV.—*Use of Heavy Motor Cars on Bridges.*—(1)— Where any person who is liable to the repair of a bridge forming part of a highway affixes or sets up, in suitable and conspicuous positions, on the bridge and in each approach to the bridge notices which, as regards all their contents or subject matter, will be clearly and distinctly legible and visible by persons approaching or being on the bridge, and as regards shape, size, colour, and all other characteristics will be clearly distinguishable from other notices placed on the bridge, and which state that the bridge is insufficient to carry a heavy motor car the registered axle-weight of any axle of which exceeds three tons or any greater weight which shall be specified in the notices, the owner of any such heavy motor car shall not cause or suffer the heavy motor car to be driven, and the person driving or in charge of the heavy motor car shall not drive the heavy motor car, upon the bridge except with the consent of the person liable to the repair of the bridge :

"Provided that where a dispute or difference arises in relation to the insufficiency of the bridge to carry any such heavy motor car, and, on a reference by the person liable to the repair of the bridge and the heavy motor car, the award or determination of an arbitrator or arbitrators or umpire adjudges the bridge to

K

be sufficient to carry a heavy motor car the registered axle-weight of any axle of which exceeds any weight specified in the notices, this Article shall cease to apply or have effect as regards any such heavy motor car, and the person liable to the repair of the bridge shall forthwith remove every notice affixed or set up in pursuance of this Article :

"Provided also that if, within a period of one month, after a request in writing by the owner of any such heavy motor car, the person liable to the repair of the bridge neglects or refuses to become a party to the submission of the dispute or difference to arbitration, or, having become a party to the submission, neglects or refuses to concur in the appointment of an arbitrator, or to appoint an arbitrator or an umpire or third arbitrator according as the submission or any agreement between the parties may require, this Article shall cease to apply or have effect so as to prohibit the driving of any such heavy motor car upon the bridge; and the person liable to the repair of the bridge shall forthwith remove every notice affixed or set up in pursuance of this Article :

"Provided further that, notwithstanding anything in the foregoing provisos, the person liable to the repair of the bridge may, in substitution for the notices previously affixed or set up, affix or set up in accordance with this Article notices specifying some axle-weight greater than that to which any award or determination mentioned in this Article has had relation ; and that thereupon this Article shall apply and have effect with respect to the substituted notices, and with respect to any other matter or thing to which this Article refers as it has applied and had effect with respect to the notices previously affixed or set up, and with respect to any such other matter or thing, prior to the affixing or setting up of the substituted notices.

"(2) The owner of a heavy motor car the axle-weight of any axle of which exceeds six tons shall not cause or suffer the heavy motor car to be driven, and the person driving or in charge of the heavy motor car shall not drive the heavy motor car upon a bridge forming part of a highway at any time when another heavy motor car, or a locomotive to which the Locomotives Act, 1898, applies, is on the bridge.

"ARTICLE XV.—*Register of Motor Cars.*—(1) The Motor Car

(Registration and Licensing) Order, 1903, shall, with the necessary modifications, apply and have effect so as to provide that for the purpose of the registration of heavy motor cars there shall be a separate part in the Register of Motor Cars, and that the separate part shall be in the Form A. set out in the Schedule to this Order or in a form to the like effect; and that to the form of particulars to be furnished by an applicant for registration of a heavy motor car, there shall, for the purpose of enabling the applicant to declare—

"(a) the weight of the heavy motor car unladen;

"(b) the axle-weight of each axle; and

"(c) the diameter of each wheel;

be added the particulars shown in the Form B. set out in the said Schedule.

"(2) In every case in which, after prior registration, the procedure prescribed by Article IV. in relation to such a case has been followed, the registering authority shall cause the entry of prior registration to be erased, and such entries as are required in compliance with the procedure prescribed by Article IV. to be made in the appropriate columns of the separate part in the Register of Motor Cars.

"ARTICLE XVI.—*Application of earlier Orders as to Motor Cars.*—As regards matters which are not herein-before expressly mentioned in relation to heavy motor cars, the Motor Car (Registration and Licensing) Order, 1903, and the Motor Cars (Use and Construction) Order, 1904, shall apply and have effect subject to the Regulations; and any provisions of either Order which are inconsistent with the Regulations shall cease to apply and have effect in relation to a heavy motor car.

"ARTICLE XVII.—*Military Motor Cars.*—The Regulations, in relation to any heavy motor car which belongs to His Majesty the King, and is used for the time being, under the care, superintendence, or control of a Secretary of State, for military purposes, shall apply and have effect—

"(a) As if, in Article III. of this Order, 'six tons' were substituted for 'five tons,' and 'eight tons' were substituted for 'six and a half tons'; and "(*b*) As if, to subdivision (1) of Article VI. of this Order, there were added the following words : that is to say,—

"'Provided further that if the tire is constructed, shod or fitted with diagonal crossbars, the conditions of this Article shall for the purpose of determining the width of the tire, apply subject to the substitution throughout those conditions of five hundred-weights for seven and a half hundredweights as the unit of regis-tered axle-weight.'

"ARTICLE XVIII.—*Short Title.*—This Order may be cited as the Heavy Motor Car Order, 1904."

EXEMPLIFICATION OF WIDTH OF TIRES

Exemplification tables, showing the minimum width required for the tire of a wheel, having regard to the diameter of the wheel, and the axle weight of the axle to which the wheel is attached.

TABLE I.

Diameter of Wheel—2 feet.
(Unit of reg. axle weight 5½ cwts.)

A.—Heavy Motor Cars.

From Tons.	From Cwts.	To Tons.	To Cwts.	Width of Tire. Inches.
	—	2	15	5
2	15	3	0½	5½
3	0½	3	6	6
3	6	3	11½	6½
3	11½	3	17	7
3	17	4	2½	7½
4	2½	4	8	8
4	8	4	13½	8½
4	13½	4	19	9
4	19	5	4½	9½
5	4½	5	10	10
5	10	5	15½	10½
5	15½	6	1	11
6	1	6	6½	11½
6	6½	6	12	12
6	12	6	17½	12½
6	17½	7	3	13
7	3	7	8½	13½
7	8½	7	14	14
7	14	7	19½	14½
7	19½	8	0	15

B.—Trailers only.

From Tons.	From Cwts.	To Tons.	To Cwts.	Width of Tire. Inches.
	—	1	13	3
1	13	1	18½	3½
1	18½	2	4	4
2	4	2	9½	4½
2	9½	2	15	5
2	15	3	0½	5½
3	0½	3	6	6
3	6	3	11½	6½
3	11½	3	17	7
3	17	4	0	7½

TABLE II.

Diameter of Wheel—2 feet 3 inches.
(Unit of reg. axle weight 6 cwts.)

A.—Heavy Motor Cars.

From Tons.	From Cwts.	To Tons.	To Cwts.	Width of Tire. Inches.
	—	3	0	5
3	0	3	6	5½
3	6	3	12	6
3	12	3	18	6½
3	18	4	4	7
4	4	4	10	7½
4	10	4	16	8
4	16	5	2	8½
5	2	5	8	9
5	8	5	14	9½
5	14	6	0	10
6	0	6	6	10½
6	6	6	12	11
6	12	6	18	11½
6	18	7	4	12
7	4	7	10	12½
7	10	7	16	13
7	16	8	0	13½

B.—Trailers only.

From Tons.	From Cwts.	To Tons.	To Cwts.	Width of Tire. Inches.
	—	1	16	3
1	16	2	2	3½
2	2	2	8	4
2	8	2	14	4½
2	14	3	0	5
3	0	3	6	5½
3	6	3	12	6
3	12	3	18	6½
3	18	4	0	7

TABLE III.

Diameter of Wheel—2 feet 6 inches.
(Unit of reg. axle weight 6½ cwts.)

A.—Heavy Motor Cars.

From (Tons)	From (Cwts.)	To (Tons)	To (Cwts.)	Width of Tire (Inches.)
	—	3	5	5
3	5	3	11½	5½
3	11½	3	18	6
3	18	4	4½	6½
4	4½	4	11	7
4	11	4	17½	7½
4	17½	5	4	8
5	4	5	10½	8½
5	10½	5	17	9
5	17	6	3½	9½
6	3½	6	10	10
6	10	6	16½	10½
6	16½	7	3	11
7	3	7	9½	11½
7	9½	7	16	12
7	16	8	0	12½

B.—Trailers only.

From (Tons)	From (Cwts.)	To (Tons)	To (Cwts.)	Width of Tire (Inches.)
	—	1	19	3
1	19	2	5½	3½
2	5½	2	12	4
2	12	2	18½	4½
2	18½	3	5	5
3	5	3	11½	5½
3	11½	3	18	6
3	18	4	0	6½

TABLE IV.

Diameter of Wheel—2 feet 9 inches.
(Unit of reg. axle weight 7 cwts.)

A.—Heavy Motor Cars.

From (Tons)	From (Cwts.)	To (Tons)	To (Cwts.)	Width of Tire (Inches.)
	—	3	10	5
3	10	3	17	5½
3	17	4	4	6
4	4	4	11	6½
4	11	4	18	7
4	18	5	5	7½
5	5	5	12	8
5	12	5	19	8½
5	19	6	6	9
6	6	6	13	9½
6	13	7	0	10
7	0	7	7	10½
7	7	7	14	11
7	14	8	0	11½

B.—Trailers only.

From (Tons)	From (Cwts.)	To (Tons)	To (Cwts.)	Width of Tire (Inches.)
	—	2	2	3
2	2	2	9	3½
2	9	2	16	4
2	16	3	3	4½
3	3	3	10	5
3	10	3	17	5½
3	17	4	0	6

TABLE V.
Diameter of Wheel—3 feet.
(Unit of reg. axle weight 7½ cwts.)

Axle Weight. From		To		Width of Tire.

A.—Heavy Motor Cars.

Tons.	Cwts.	Tons.	Cwts.	Inches.
	—	3	15	5
3	15	4	2½	5½
4	2½	4	10	6
4	10	4	17½	6½
4	17½	5	5	7
5	5	5	12½	7½
5	12½	6	0	8
6	0	6	7½	8½
6	7½	6	15	9
6	15	7	2½	9½
7	2½	7	10	10
7	10	7	17½	10½
7	17½	8	0	11

B.—Trailers only.

Tons.	Cwts.	Tons.	Cwts.	Inches.
	—	2	5	3
2	5	2	12½	3½
2	12½	3	0	4
3	0	3	7½	4½
3	7½	3	15	5
3	15	4	0	5½

TABLE VI.
Diameter of Wheel—3 feet 3 inches.
(Unit of reg. axle weight 7¾ cwts.)

Axle Weight. From		To		Width of Tire.

A.—Heavy Motor Cars.

Tons.	Cwts.	Tons.	Cwts.	Inches.
	—	3	17½	5
3	17½	4	5¼	5½
4	5¼	4	13	6
4	13	5	0¾	6½
5	0¾	5	8½	7
5	8½	5	16¼	7½
5	16¼	6	4	8
6	4	6	11¾	8½
6	11¾	6	19½	9
6	19½	7	7¼	9½
7	7¼	7	15	10
7	15	8	0	10½

B.—Trailers only.

Tons.	Cwts.	Tons.	Cwts.	Inches.
	—	2	6½	3
2	6½	2	14¼	3½
2	14¼	3	2	4
3	2	3	9¾	4½
3	9¾	3	17½	5
3	17½	4	0	5½

TABLE VII.
Diameter of Wheel—3 feet 6 inches.
(Unit of reg. axle weight 8 cwts.)

Axle Weight. From		To		Width of Tire.

A.—Heavy Motor Cars.

Tons.	Cwts.	Tons.	Cwts.	Inches.
	—	4	0	5
4	0	4	8	5½
4	8	4	16	6
4	16	5	4	6½
5	4	5	12	7
5	12	6	0	7½
6	0	6	8	8
6	8	6	16	8½
6	16	7	4	9
7	4	7	12	9½
7	12	8	0	10

B.—Trailers only.

Tons.	Cwts.	Tons.	Cwts.	Inches.
	—	2	8	3
2	8	2	16	3½
2	16	3	4	4
3	4	3	12	4½
3	12	4	0	5

TABLE VIII.
Diameter of Wheel—3 feet 9 inches.
(Unit of reg. axle wheel 8¼ cwts.)

Axle Weight. From		To		Width of Tire.

A.—Heavy Motor Cars.

Tons.	Cwts.	Tons.	Cwts.	Inches.
	—	4	2½	5
4	2½	4	10¾	5½
4	10¾	4	19	6
4	19	5	7¼	6½
5	7¼	5	15½	7
5	15½	6	3¾	7½
6	3¾	6	12	8
6	12	7	0¼	8½
7	0¼	7	8½	9
7	8½	7	16¾	9½
7	16¾	8	0	10

B.—Trailers only.

Tons.	Cwts.	Tons.	Cwts.	Inches.
	—	2	9½	3
2	9½	2	17¾	3½
2	17¾	3	6	4
3	6	3	14¼	4½
3	14¼	4	0	5

TABLE IX.
Diameter of Wheel—4 feet.
(Unit of reg. axle weight 8½ cwts.)

A.—Heavy Motor Cars.

From Tons.	Cwts.	To Tons.	Cwts.	Width of Tire. Inches.
—		4	5	5
4	5	4	13½	5½
4	13½	5	2	6
5	2	5	10½	6½
5	10½	5	19	7
5	19	6	7½	7½
6	7½	6	16	8
6	16	7	4½	8½
7	4½	7	13	9
7	13	8	0½	9½

B.—Trailers only.

From Tons.	Cwts.	To Tons.	Cwts.	Inches.
—		2	11	3
2	11	2	19½	3½
2	19½	3	8	4
3	8	3	16½	4½
3	16½	4	0	5

TABLE X.
Diameter of Wheel—4 feet 3 inches.
(Unit of reg. axle weight 8¾ cwts.)

A.—Heavy Motor Cars.

From Tons.	Cwts.	To Tons.	Cwts.	Width of Tire. Inches.
—		4	7½	5
4	7½	4	16¼	5½
4	16¼	5	5	6
5	5	5	13¾	6½
5	13¾	6	2½	7
6	2½	6	11¼	7½
6	11¼	7	0	8
7	0	7	8¾	8½
7	8¾	7	17½	9
7	17½	8	0	9½

B.—Trailers only.

From Tons.	Cwts.	To Tons.	Cwts.	Inches.
—		2	12½	3
2	12½	3	1¼	3½
3	1¼	3	10	4
3	10	3	18¾	4½
3	18¾	4	0	5

TABLE XI.
Diameter of Wheel—4 feet 6 inches.
(Unit of reg. axle weight 9 cwts.)

A.—Heavy Motor Cars.

From Tons.	Cwts.	To Tons.	Cwts.	Width of Tire. Inches.
—		4	10	5
4	10	4	19	5½
4	19	5	8	6
5	8	5	17	6½
5	17	6	6	7
6	6	6	15	7½
6	15	7	4	8
7	4	7	13	8½
7	13	8	0	9

B.—Trailers only.

From Tons.	Cwts.	To Tons.	Cwts.	Inches.
—		2	14	3
2	14	3	3	3½
3	3	3	12	4
3	12	4	0	4½

TABLE XII.
Diameter of Wheel—4 feet 9 inches.
(Unit of reg. axle weight 9¼ cwts.)

A.—Heavy Motor Cars.

From Tons.	Cwts.	To Tons.	Cwts.	Width of Tire. Inches.
—		4	12½	5
4	12½	5	1¾	5½
5	1¾	5	11	6
5	11	6	0¼	6½
6	0¼	6	9½	7
6	9½	6	18¾	7½
6	18¾	7	8	8
7	8	7	17¼	8½
7	17¼	8	0	9

B.—Trailers only.

From Tons.	Cwts.	To Tons.	Cwts.	Inches.
—		2	15½	3
2	15½	3	4¾	3½
3	4¾	3	14	4
3	14	4	0	4½

TABLE XIII.

Diameter of Wheel—5 feet.
(Unit of reg. axle weight 9½ cwts.)

| Axle Weight. | | Width of Tire. |
| From | To | |

A.—Heavy Motor Cars.

Tons.	Cwts.	Tons.	Cwts.	Inches.
	—	4	15	5
4	15	5	4½	5½
5	4½	5	14	6
5	14	6	3½	6½
6	3½	6	13	7
6	13	7	2½	7½
7	2½	7	12	8
7	12	8	0	8½

B.—Trailers only.

Tons.	Cwts.	Tons.	Cwts.	Inches.
	—	2	17	3
2	17	3	6½	3½
3	6½	3	16	4
3	16	4	0	4½

TABLE XIV.

Diameter of Wheel—5 feet 3 inches.
(Unit of reg. axle weight 9¾ cwts.)

| Axle Weight. | | Width of Tire. |
| From | To | |

A.—Heavy Motor Cars.

Tons.	Cwts.	Tons.	Cwts.	Inches.
	—	4	17½	5
4	17½	5	7¼	5½
5	7¼	5	17	6
5	17	6	6¾	6½
6	6¾	6	16½	7
6	16½	7	6¼	7½
7	6¼	7	16	8
7	16	8	0	8½

B.—Trailers only.

Tons.	Cwts.	Tons.	Cwts.	Inches.
	—	2	18½	3
2	18½	3	8¼	3½
3	8¼	3	18	4
3	18	4	0	4½

TABLE XV.

Diameter of Wheel—5 feet 6 inches.
(Unit of reg. axle weight 10 cwts.)

| Axle Weight. | | Width of Tire. |
| From | To | |

A.—Heavy Motor Cars.

Tons.	Cwts.	Tons.	Cwts.	Inches.
	—	5	0	5
5	0	5	10	5½
5	10	6	0	6
6	0	6	10	6½
6	10	7	0	7
7	0	7	10	7½
7	10	8	0	8

B.—Trailers only.

Tons.	Cwts.	Tons.	Cwts.	Inches.
	—	3	0	3
3	0	3	10	3½
3	10	4	0	4

MOTOR *v.* HORSE HAULAGE

ACTUAL RESULTS CONTRASTED

THE following log (shown on opposite page) is supplied by Messrs. Ley & Sons, Millers, Walton-le-Dale, near Preston. The wagon employed is a "Leyland," Class B. The conditions of working in comparison with horse haulage are probably the worst possible from an economic point of view. Ninety-five per cent of the work done is between the docks and the mill or the warehouse, returning to the docks empty. The road from the docks for three-quarters of a mile is cobble in wretched condition, and a more difficult road for motor vehicles could not be imagined. There is also a gradient, fairly long, of 1 in 10. The maximum load carried is 50 sacks of 240 lb., say, $5\frac{1}{2}$ tons.

The following is furnished by the Londonderry firm as supplied by one of their customers. North-country roads in bad condition; steepest gradient 1 in 7.

January, 1904.

Based on 897 ton-miles = 6 days' running.

	£	s.	d.
Depreciation and interest per week . .	1	12	6
Driver	1	16	0
Fireman	1	4	0
Third man assisting delivery . . .	1	0	0
Coke at 8d. per cwt.	0	10	8
Oil and sundries	0	9	0
[1] Set aside for repairs	0	15	0
	£7	7	2

£7. 7s. 2d. ÷ 897 ton-miles = slightly under 2d. per ton-mile.

[1] The amount set aside for repairs should be a good deal increased, especially when the wagon is heavily worked, six days to the week.—*Author.*

MOTOR.

	£	s.	d.
Prime cost, £500.			
Interest on capital at 5 % .	25	0	0
Driver at 30s. per week .	78	0	0
Loader at 20s. ,, .	52	0	0
Coke at 12s. per ton . .	38	0	0
Oil, water, and sundries .	20	0	0
Repairs (absolute cost aver- aged over two years) .	50	0	0
Depreciation at 15 % on prime cost . .	75	0	0
	£338	0	0

Daily mileage and work, 6.30 *a.m. to*
5.30 *p.m.*

Mill to warehouse,	45 sacks,	1½ miles.
Warehouse to docks,	light,	2 ,,
Docks to mill,	50 sacks,	3½ ,,
Mill to warehouse,	45 ,,	1½ ,,
Warehouse to docks,	light,	2 ,,
Docks to mill,	50 sacks,	3½ ,,
Mill to docks,	light,	3½ ,,
Docks to mill,	50 sacks,	3½ ,,
Mill to docks,	light,	3½ ,,
Docks to mill,	50 sacks,	3½ ,,

Total miles per day, loaded = 17
,,   ,,   ,, light = 11
Total mileage = 28

Dealing with 290 sacks of 240 lb.
weight per day.

Cost performed by horses = £10. 4s. 2d.
per week.

Cost performed by motor = £6. 10s. 0d.

Saving per week by ,, £3. 14s. 2d.

HORSES.

Daily mileage and work of 2 *horses,*
wagon, and man, 7 *a.m. to* 6 *p.m.*

Mill to warehouse,	30 sacks,	1½ miles.
Warehouse to docks,	light,	2 ,,
Docks to mill,	25 sacks,	3½ ,,
Mill to docks,	light,	3½ ,,
Docks to mill,	25 sacks,	3½ ,,
Mill to docks,	light,	3½ ,,
Docks to mill,	25 sacks,	3½ ,,

Total miles per day, loaded = 12
,,   ,,   ,, light = 9
Total mileage = 21

Dealing with 105 sacks of 240 lb.
weight per day.

The hire of horses is 7s. 6d. per day
each, equal to 1d. per sack 1½ miles
and 2d. per sack 3½ miles.

6 horses, 3 wagons, 3 men will cart from
20 to 30 sacks more per day than
the motor from docks to mill.
The cost therefore of hauling the
same quantity as the motor would
be £10. 4s. 2d. per week.

Messrs. Robertson, Fleetwood, furnish the following account of a run of their standard 5-ton wagon. It is interesting as demonstrating very conclusively the advantages of motor versus horse traction, the one being run against the other for trial experiment.

"Left London on Monday at 9 a.m. with trailer, arriving at destination at 1.30 p,m. ; loading with 7 ton 10 cwt. of furniture occupied till 6 p.m. Journeyed to Watford, 8¾ miles, same evening. Wagon under steam 13 hours, consuming 6½ cwt. of coke. Left Watford next morning at 7.30, taking a 1 in 9 hill *en route*, and arrived at end of journey at 2 p.m. After unloading returned to London (Messrs. Shoolbred's), arriving 9.30 p.m. Total journey covered second day being 47½ miles and net running time 8 hours 50 minutes. The round journey was 82¼ miles. The wagon on second day was under steam 15 hours and consumed 7¾ cwt. of coke."

As against the above the same journey was commenced on the Tuesday morning by two of Messrs. Shoolbred's own 3-horse vans having 3 horses to each van, and moving practically the same load, viz. 7½ tons. They arrived back at 9.30 p.m. on Thursday night, having been 3 days and 2 nights out. Put briefly and accurately, the wagon with 2 men did in 2 days what 2 vans with 6 horses did in 3 days. In going up the 1 in 9 hill with the horses each van had to be hauled up alternately by the combined efforts of 6 horses.

As a result of this run Messrs. Shoolbred purchased the wagon. The nature of the work does not lend itself to record running or low consumption of fuel on account of the time standing loading and unloading under steam ; but below is given a month's working, which is a fair average, and notwithstanding the disadvantages, the fuel consumption is very low.

Date.	Character of work—furniture removal, etc.	With Trailer.	Miles run.	Load in tons.	Ton-miles.	Hours under steam.	Hours running.	Coke used in 100 lb. bags.
April 25	Streatham and Euston Station (2)	Yes	7½	6¼	46·87 }	12	4	2½
,, 25	,, ,, ,,	,,	7½	3½	26·25 }			
,, 26	To Tunbridge Wells .	,,	42	8¼	346·6	13	10½	13
,, 27	,, ,, ,,	,,	40	2¼	90	14	8½	6
,, 28	Shad Thames, etc.	No	5	6 }	30	9	3	3
,, 28	,, ,,	,,	5	Light }				
,, 29	Streatham and Euston Station (2)	Yes	15	10¾	80·74	11	4	3
,, 30	Washing and cleaning	—	—	—	—	—	—	—
May 2	To Aston Rawton	Yes	42	8¼	346·5	14½	12	9
,, 3	At ,, ,,	,,	5½	8¼	45·38 }	11	3	3
,, 3	,, ,, ,,	,,	5½	1	5·5 }			
,, 4	From Ashton to London	,,	42	2¼	94·5	10	8	7
,, 5	To Bromley and West Kensington	,,	15	9¼	138·75 }	16	8½	6
,, 5	,, ,, ,,	,,	15	3	45·0 }			
,, 6	Shad Thames and Euston .	No	5	6	30·0 }			
,, 6	,, ,, ,,	,,	5	Light	— }	11	4½	4
,, 6	,, ,, ,,	,,	2	½	1·0 }			
,, 6	,, ,, ,,	,,	2	1½	3·0 }			
,, 7	Streatham .	Yes	7½	6¼	46·87 }	7	4	4
,, 7	,, .	,,	7½	2¼	16·87 }			
,, 9	Finsbury and Highbury	,,	8	11¼	90·0 }	14	5	4
,, 9	,, ,, ,,	,,	8	2¼	18·0 }			
,, 10	To Weybridge and return	,,	24	8¾	210·0 }	18	12	9
,, 10	,, ,, ,,	,,	24	3	72·0 }			
,, 11	Millwall, etc.	,,	8	6¼	50·0 }	10½	3	3
,, 11	,, ,,	,,	8	2¼	18·0 }			
,, 12	Weybridge and return	,,	24	9	216·0 }	18	12	10
,, 12	,, ,, ,,	,,	24	2¼	54·0 }			
,, 13	Shad Thames and Euston .	No	10	8¼	41·25	9	3	2
,, 14	Cleaning, etc.	—	—	—	—			
,, 16	Caledonian Rd. and Hampstead (2)	Yes	10	9	45·0	11	4½	2
,, 17	To Basingstoke .	,,	46	3	138·0	14	12½	9
,, 18	Basingstoke to Winchester .	,,	24	3	72·0	8	6	5
,, 19	Winchester to Staines	,,	52	8¼	420·0	15	13	10
,, 20	From Staines	,,	20	8¼	165·0	12	5	5
,, 21	Cleaning, etc.	—	—	—	—	—	—	—
,, 24	To Bexley .	No	17	6¾	114·76	11	7	5
			583	177	3126·73	269	153	124½

The working cost of above, based on an average rate of wages, works out as follows :—

	£	s.	d.
Interest on £550 at 5 per cent . . .	2	5	10
Driver's wages at 36s. per week . . .	7	4	0
Fireman's wages at 24s. per week .	4	16	0
111 cwt. of coke at 9d. per cwt. . .	4	3	3
Oil, grease, waste, and firewood . .	1	4	4
Allowance for repairs . . .	4	0	0
Depreciation at 15 per cent per annum, say .	6	10	0
	£30	3	5

This works out at 2·31d. per ton-mile.

One cwt. of coke averaged 2·4 hours for the wagon under steam.

APPENDIX

FIRST LIVERPOOL TRIALS, 1898

SUMMARY OF PARTICULARS OF COMPETING WAGONS

	LIFU (No. 1).	THORNYCROFT (No. 3). 6 wheels.	THORNYCROFT (No. 4).	LEYLAND (No. 5).
Dimensions over all—Length, breadth, and height	16′ 2″ × 6′ 6″ 9′ 0″	25′ 2″ × 6′ 6″ 10′ 5″	16′ 0″ × 6′ 6″ 10′ 5″	17′ 9″ × 6′ 5″ 10′ 6″
Extreme dimensions of platform	10′ 2″ × 6′ 2″	17′ 10″ × 6″ 6″	9′ 3″ × 6′ 6″	12′ 7″ × 5′ 10½″
Ratio of available platform area to extreme moving area .	0·59	0·73	0·58	0·61
Diameter of wheels in inches .	32 and 34	33, 39, and 43½	33 and 39	37
Width of tyres in inches . .	3	4½ and 4¾	4½ and 4¾	4 and 5
Height of platform when loaded in inches	38½	48½	46¾	42½
Mean deflection of springs under load in inches. . . .	2½	2½	1¼	2½
Wheel base	10′ 7″ × 5′ 9″	11′ 1″ × 5′ 9½″	7′ 2″ × 5′ 5½″	10′ 2″ × 5′ 7″
Angle of lock in degrees . .	35	36	36	34
Boiler—Heating surface . .	80	65	65	110
Declared working pressure. Pounds per square inch .	210	175	175	200
Grate area in square feet .	—	2½	—	—
Engine—Cylinder stroke in inches	3 and 6 5	4 and 7 5	4 and 7 5	3 and 5 6
Revolutions per min. full speed	600	500	500	500
Declared B.H.P. . . .	20	18	18	14
Gearing—Ratio between engine shaft and driving wheels	8 to 1	9 and 12 to 1	8 to 1	8, 13½, and 28 to 1
Distance capacity— Fuel. In miles	70·2	12·6	26·1	37·9
Water. In miles . . .	29·7	5·5	13·9	13·5
Load carried in tons . . .	2·20	4·73	2·53	4·06
Tare—Without fuel, water, or stores. In tons . . .	2·39	3·85	2·83	2·86
Fully provisioned (not including attendants). In tons	3·29	4·77	3·62	3·32
Mean tare (not including attendants) in tons . .	2·67	4·41	3·26	3·15
Total moving weight — Laden and fully provisioned (including attendants). In tons	5·34	9·55	6·16	7·43
Mean total moving weight in tons	4·94	9·25	5·91	7·29
Ratio of mean tare to load . .	1·21	0·93	1·29	0·78
Ratio of mean total moving weight to load . . .	2·25	1·96	2·34	1·80
Mean tare per declared B.H.P. in cwts.	2·67	4·90	3·18	4·50
Mean total moving weight per declared B.H.P. in cwts. .	4·94	10·28	6·84	10·61

FIRST LIVERPOOL TRIALS (1898)

SUMMARY OF PARTICULARS OF COMPETING WAGONS—*Continued*

	LIFU (No. 1).	THORNYCROFT (No. 3). 6 wheels.	THORNYCROFT (No. 4).	LEYLAND (No. 5).
Declared distribution of weight on wheels in tons—				
Light and without fuel or water—				
Steering wheels	1·433	1·581	1·472	1·600
Driving wheels	·955	1·523	1·353	1·263
Trailing wheels	—	·748	—	
Running order (without attendants)—				
Steering wheels	1·646	1·781	1·810	—
Driving wheels	1·646	2·042	1·805	No records
Trailing wheels	—	·947	—	—
Laden and provisioned (including attendants). Load equally distributed over platform—				
Steering wheels	1·201	1·781	1·423	—
Driving wheels	4·139	4·377	4·734	No records
Trailing wheels	—	3·393	—	—

COST OF WORKING BASED ON PERFORMANCES DURING THE 1898 LIVERPOOL TRIALS

In tabulating results the judges proceeded under three working conditions, viz.—

Table.	Distance covered per 10-hour day.	
	Loaded.	Unloaded.
1	35 miles	—
. 2	Speed × 10	—
3	Speed × 5	Speed × 5

Difficulties were encountered in working out the cost and establishing comparative data, extremes of speed and weight being included in one class, and the basis was taken of the commercial speed in miles multiplied by 10 working hours per day, these figures being deemed to establish what could best be accepted as of commercial consideration, and all additions or allowances were made with this view in mind. At the same time, the tests having only extended over four days, it was impossible to judge of the endurance capabilities, which after all are of supreme importance, and such working costs could only be accepted as correct provided similar conditions were kept up day after day in regular working.

In Tables 1 and 2 it is presumed that a vehicle can travel between two fixed points with a full load both ways, as in such cases as between two warehouses or factories, ship and warehouse, or where any sustained haulage could be so dealt with.

Table 3 is based on what might reasonably be supposed to be extreme conditions and likely only to appertain in urban haulage, where only half the total ton-miles are obtainable, and the judges were of opinion that an omnibus service might be taken as one-fourteenth of the net ton-miles in Table 3.

The net time occupied in actual running divided into the whole distance travelled gives the speed. Analysis was also made of the speeds made between many of the timing places, and due regard was paid to uniform running of the competing vehicles as to their capabilities.

Delays from all causes, therefore, were deducted where they were such as would not hinder working on commercial lines, e.g. a stoppage for luncheon; but all stoppages for incidental attentions in the way to fittings, mechanism, boilers, or other reasons likely to be encountered day by day in actual commercial work, were included in the time necessary to complete the journeys.

From the gross time, therefore, to determine the "commercial duration" of the runs was deducted the time spent (*a*) on errors of route, (*b*) in making exceptional repairs, (*c*) at the depôts *en route*, (*d*) one minute for each official stoppage on hills.

Additional allowance was made of one-half the time occupied by Thornycroft's six-wheeled vehicle, which was subjected to inordinate delays in having to pick up water in the country at points where no official arrangements had been made.

Fifteen minutes were added to the time thus obtained for each intermediate depôt.

The product represents the best "commercial duration" of each journey procurable, and this gives the "commercial speed" after division into the distance travelled, and the average of these speeds for the runs completed respectively was the speed accepted in calculating the figures in the tabulated records subsequently to be herein set out. The speeds thus fixed were lower than those made during some of the runs; and but for pronouncedly faulty wheels better speeds would undoubtedly have been made generally.

The weight carried plus the distance travelled represented ton-miles of load.

To the weights actually carried was added (1) proportionate weight of the average quantity of water unconsumed above what was needed for an additional 3 miles at each of the depôts *en route* and at the end of each run; (2) the weight of coal or oil above what was needed for an additional 3 miles unconsumed at end of each journey.

Depreciation and Maintenance.—In the absence of experience no reliable figures could be derived from the trials, and the judges allowed 15 per cent per annum for depreciation on the prime cost of the vehicles.

Maintenance was estimated as equal to 20 to 30 per cent per annum on vehicle prime cost, according to construction, speed, and daily mileage. The "Leyland" was taken at a higher percentage, owing to what was considered the inadequate amount which its low prime cost afforded when compared equally with the others.

Labour and material were included under "maintenance," and the figures must be viewed in conjunction with the depreciation rate. It was considered whether, having in view the discarding of vehicles after, say, five years, with expenditure on repairs in meanwhile; or a longer life, with such repairs needful for such prolongation of life, that 35 per cent per annum on prime cost, where running on sett and mixed pavements, would be required to cover "depreciation and maintenance," however apportioned, where a ten-hour working day was the rule; but when running on good macadam or like roads such a percentage might be reduced.

L

On the other hand, working under particularly uneven setts or similar uncommon circumstances an increase would be necessary.

Fuel and Water.—Consumption of these given in the subsequent tables were first subjected to allowances where exceptional influences were operating during the competition. When vehicles were proceeding unloaded the consumption quantities stated for work thus done are estimated as two-thirds of the consumption when fully loaded. It was stated that probably the true consumptions would be "proportional to the total moving weights plus constants peculiar to each vehicle for the frictional losses of the mechanism and the rolling resistances at the same speeds"; but no records were taken without loads, the above estimated ratio for light loads was assumed.

Water was estimated as costing 1s. per 1000 gallons. The water consumptions were not, however, evaporative results, except in the case of No. 1, but the actual quantities used to perform the several journeys.

The liquid fuel used on the "Lifu" and the "Leyland" was the ordinary refined petroleum oil or kerosene. The large amount used on the "Lifu" was probably owing to the great rate of speed maintained.

The "Thornycroft" vehicles were coal fired and hand stoked.

The application of oil fuel for steam generation on the "Lifu" and "Leyland" was of so simple a character that the whole management of running these vehicles could be easily undertaken by one man. No special arrangements were made for automatic or other convenient method of stoking on the "Thornycrofts," rendering apparently an additional attendant necessary and thereby considerably increasing cost of working.

Sundry Charges.—The amounts charged to rent, rates, and taxes might be much reduced where shed accommodation could be obtained, except, perhaps, in case of the large six-wheeled "Thornycroft."

Appended is a summary of the performances of the four vehicles during the trials:—

LOG SHEETS' SUMMARY

	LIFU.	THORNYCROFT (6-wheeler).	THORNYCROFT (4-wheeler).	LEYLAND.
Maximum steam pressure—				
Pounds per square inch	250	170	190	240
Minimum steam pressure—				
Pounds per square inch	175	70	110	100
Average of observations	206	125	152	175
Stoppages—	No. Duration.	No. Duration.	No. Duration.	No. Duration.
Regulation	15 = 4h. 18m.	16 = 4h. 20m.	21 = 3h. 14m.	11 = 3h. 38m.
To make repairs	2 = 0h. 10m.	17 = 6h. 36m.	5 = 6h. 24m.	5 = 3h. 54m.
Other causes	3 = 0h. 12m.	28 = 5h. 37m.	5 = 0h. 18m.	6 = 0h. 23m.
Total distance travelled. Miles	143·5	107·4	143	95·9
Distance accepted	143·5	71·8	143	71·5
Oil consumed	96 gals.	—	—	37·5 gals.
Coal (and coke) consumed	—	2247 lbs.	1441 lbs.	—
Water consumed	666 gals.	1029½ gals.	558 gals.	384 gals.
Commercial duration of total distance run	20 h. 26 m.	25 h. 43 m.	27 h. 23 m.	16 h. 4 m.
Average of total moving weights	5·340 tons	9·551	6·157	7·426
Average of mean moving weights	4·939 tons	9·254	5·911	7·289
Factors affecting the cost per net ton mile—				
Prime cost	£524	£750	£630	£375
Speed—Actual running	8·29 M.P.H.	3·41 M.P.H.	5·98 M.P.H.	5·25 M.P.H.
Commercial	7·02 M.P.H.	2·79 M.P.H.	5·22 M.P.H.	4·45 M.P.H.
Load carried in tons	2·20	4·73	2·53 M.P.H.	4·06 M.P.H.
Time occupied in obtaining the declared working pressure	20 m.	23 m.	21 m.	22 m.
Fuel consumption to raise steam	1·0 gal.	65 lbs.	64 lbs.	¾ gal.
,, ,, per vehicle mile	0·655 gal.	19·07 lbs.	9·20 lbs.	0·528 gal.
,, ,, per ton-mile	0·298 gal.	4·03 lbs.	3·64 lbs.	0·130 gal.
Water consumption—				
Per vehicle mile	4·54 gals.	9·11 gals.	3·69 gals.	3·41 gals.
Per ton-mile	2·06 gals.	1·93 gals.	1·46 gal.	0·84 gal.
Motive power per ton-mile of load	1·22d.	0·36d.	0·32d.	0·53d.
Comparative working costs.				
Table 1—	35 miles per day, laden.	35 miles per day, laden.	35 miles per day, laden.	35 miles per day, laden.
Annual expenditure	£433. 2s. 10d.	£553. 10s. 7d.	£447. 0s. 1d.	£367. 12s. 9d.
Work done. Net ton-miles per annum	20,020	43,043	23,023	36,946
Cost per net ton-mile	5·19d.	3·09d.	4·66d.	2·39d.
Table 2—	70 miles per day, laden.	28 miles per day, laden.	52 miles per day, laden.	44 miles per day, laden.
Annual expenditure	£589. 1s.	£521.18s.11d.	£495. 7s. 9d.	£407. 7s. 5d.
Work done. Net ton-miles per annum	40,040	34,434	34,206	46,446
Cost per net ton-mile	3·53d.	3·64d.	3·48d.	2·10d.
Table 3—	35 miles per day, laden. Do. do., light.	14 miles per day, laden. Do. do., light.	26 miles per day, laden. Do. do., light.	22 miles per day, laden. Do. do., light.
Annual expenditure	£555. 5s.	£513. 7s. 9d.	£487. 16s.	£380.17s.11d.
Work done. Net ton-miles per annum	20,020	17·217	17·103	23,223
Cost per net ton-mile	6·66d.	7·16d.	6·84d.	3·94d.

AWARDS

First prize, £100.   The Lancashire Steam Motor
                     Co., Leyland, near Preston   " Leyland."
Second prize, £75.   The Liquid Fuel Engineering
                     Co., Ltd., East Cowes, Isle
                     of Wight   .   .   .   .   " Lifu."
Third prize, £50.   The   Steam   Carriage   and
                     Wagon Co., Ltd., Chiswick   " Thornycroft "
                                                 (4-wheeler).

Each vehicle had merits and defects of its own, and all showed
great ingenuity and skill in attempting compliance with the
conditions of the competition.   The prizes were awarded by the
judges on what they considered the general comparative merits
of the vehicles in competition.

REMARKS ON 1898 LIVERPOOL TRIALS

The " Particulars of Competition " made it clear that the chief
factors determining merits were to be economy of working, load
carried, general control, and manœuvring capabilities.   No. 3
(Thornycroft's six-wheeler), which was regarded as not being
adapted to the traffic intended, was excluded.   The deductions to
be drawn from the trials were :—

Town Haulage.—Vehicles were capable of replacing horse
haulage with economy for a number of trade purposes in Liverpool and district.

Distance Haulage.—Vehicles could economically compete for
carriage of loads up to 4 tons, over such distances embraced by
the trials (30 to 40 miles), where the rates were equal to those
of the Liverpool district.

Volume of Traffic.—That there were opportunities for the
establishment of carrying undertakings and adoption of such
vehicles by individual firms.

Further Limitation.—The calculated costs per net ton-mile
showed a saving on current railway rates, but that motor vehicles

could not successfully compete for traffic in opposition to reduced railway rates except under special circumstances.

Maintenance and Efficiency.—Whilst it was demonstrated under test of actual working, of great severity, that new vehicles might work in commercial competition with railway rates with loads up to 4 tons, and over distances of from 30 to 40 miles, the severity of the duties motor vehicles had to perform in carrying heavy loads at useful speeds on common roads was so great as to involve even greater maintenance and depreciation charges than those used in the calculations, which would thereby increase cost of working and render the service in a measure uncertain. That motor vehicles in the then stage of development were liable to temporary breakdowns which might cause considerable delay and annoyance.

Effect on Roads.—That the imperfections of common roads were the principal causes of the heavy maintenance and depreciation charges and of the element of uncertainty. That on good macadam roads with moderate gradients the vehicles to which prizes were awarded would do good service with the respective loads carried during trials, but none of them could be relied upon for a regular service on roads such as the routes selected for competition.

That it was anticipated that the consumption of fuel and water might be very considerably increased when the vehicles had to run over wet, muddy, or exceptionally heavy roads, but as such conditions would be accidental they would probably not materially alter average cost per ton-mile.

Wheels.—That the wheels and tyres adopted by all the manufacturers were probably perfectly efficient as carriers, but were all structurally more or less inefficient as drivers.

Manœuvring.—That none of the vehicles were able to manœuvre into and out of an embayment as effectively and rapidly as might be expected when time and experience had effected improvements in design, but they were capable of going anywhere that horse-drawn vehicles were ordinarily required to go.

Control.—That the same was at least as good as with the best types of horse-drawn vehicles.

Hill-climbing.—The hill-climbing powers compared with horse-drawn vehicles were much superior when commercial efficiency was considered. That at least two speeds or an equivalent were essential to successful working on common roads with steep or even average gradients.

Driving Operations.—That motor vehicles to attain wider adoption must be made more automatic in regulating and driving, to enable comparatively unskilled attendants to undertake their management.

Experience.—That the experience gained during the trials would undoubtedly tend to obviate some of the chief causes of the troubles which arose on the road.

In future competitions it was advocated that trials be made both when loaded and when light, and conditions regulating future trials should be published at least eight months previous to the intended trials.

GENERAL REMARKS

(1) The lessons to be derived from the trials, besides the remedying of the defects in the vehicles shown in the running, were that the tyres were insufficiently secured to withstand the hammering and strains occasioned by the granite setts encountered, and that the forms of tyres and wheels employed by the makers, though no doubt sufficient to carry the loads, were inadequate as drivers. At the conclusion of even the second day's run some of the wheel-spokes and all the tyres showed considerable signs of straining.

(2) Practical absolute control of the vehicles on orders being given to stop when descending hills. No feature was more evidenced than the prompt manner in which such stops were made.

(3) Apart from differences in design, the successful manœuvring of the vehicles naturally varied with the proficiency of the operators in handling. All competitors chose to back into the embayment, such as horse vehicles are generally handled, but there was no reason why motor vehicles should follow suit.

SECOND LIVERPOOL TRIALS, 1899

SUMMARY OF PARTICULARS OF COMPETING VEHICLES

	Thornycroft (No. 1).	Thornycroft (No. 2).	Coulthard (No. 3).	Leyland (No. 5).	Clarkson and Capel (No. 6).	Bayley (No. 9).
Dimensions over all—Length, breadth, and height	16′ 0″ × 6′ 6″ 8′ 5″	32′ 6″ × 6′ 6″ 9′ 0″	15′ 7″ × 6′ 6″ 9′ 4″	18′ 2″ × 6′ 5″ 10′ 1″	17′ 9″ × 6′ 5″ 10′ 10″	16′ 5″ × 6′ 6″ 8′ 7″
Dimensions of level platform	10′ 0″ × 6′ 6″	12′ $0\frac{1}{2}$″ × 5′ $7\frac{1}{2}$″ 10′ $5\frac{1}{2}$″ × 5′ 6″	10′ 5″ × 5′ 5″	12′ 6 × 5′ 8″	11′ 0″ × 6′ 4″	9′ $2\frac{1}{2}$″ × 6′ $2\frac{1}{2}$″
Ratio of available platform area to extreme moving area in any horizontal plane	0·58	0·59	0·56	0·60	0·61	0·56
Diameter of wheels. Inches	33 and 39	34 and 39 32 and 35	$33\frac{1}{2}$ and $35\frac{1}{2}$	39	38 and 41	$32\frac{1}{2}$ and 35
Width of tyres. Inches	$4\frac{3}{8}$ and $5\frac{1}{4}$	$4\frac{1}{4}$ and $5\frac{1}{4}$ 3	4 and 5	4 and 5	$4\frac{1}{2}$	$4\frac{1}{8}$ and $5\frac{1}{4}$
Height of Platform. Loaded	$43\frac{3}{4}$	45 42	$42\frac{1}{2}$	43	$45\frac{1}{2}$	42
Mean deflection of springs under load. Inches	$1\frac{3}{4}$	2 $1\frac{1}{2}$	$2\frac{1}{2}$	$2\frac{1}{2}$	$2\frac{1}{2}$	$2\frac{1}{2}$
Angle of lock. Degrees.	34	35	30	26	31	25
Boiler—Heating surface. Square feet	83	83	77	110	80	70
Declared working pressure. Pounds per square inch	175	200	212	200	200	200
Engine—Revolutions per minute full speed	770	770	500	400	600	500
Cylinders and stroke	4 and 7 5	4 and 7 5	$2\frac{3}{4}$, $4\frac{1}{8}$, and 6 5	$2\frac{3}{4}$ and 5 6	$2\frac{3}{4}$ and 6 4	4 and 7 5
Declared B.H.P.	35	40	14	14	14	22
Ratio of gearing between engine shaft and driving wheels	10·1 and 17·7	10·1 and 17·7	7, 11·5, and 19·5	8·5, 15·25, and 35	12 and 36	8·4 and 13·7
Distance capacity—Fuel. Miles	37·8	51·7	—	37·1	41·4	49·7
Water. Miles	15·9	16·3	—	12·5	23·0	17·6
Load carried. Tons	3·73	4·09 2·56	2·32	4·44	3·35	3·67

SECOND LIVERPOOL TRIALS (1899)

SUMMARY OF PARTICULARS OF COMPETING VEHICLES—*continued*

	Thornycroft (No. 1).	Thornycroft (No. 2).	Coulthard (No. 3).	Leyland (No. 5).	Clarkson and Capel (No. 6).	Bayley (No. 9).
Tare—Without food, water, or stores. Tons	2·996	3·167 / 0·737	2·238	2·850	2·996	2·966
Fully provisioned (not including attendants). Tons	3·812	4·330 / 0·737	2·636	3·258	3·448	3·622
Mean (not including attendants). Tons	3·582	4·004 / 0·737	2·524	3·141	3·359	3·469
Total moving weight—Laden and fully provisioned (including attendants). Tons	7·465	8·420 / 3·182	4·998	7·753	6·765	7·282
Mean do. do. Tons	7·235	8·094 / 3·182	4·886	7·636	6·676	7·129
Ratio of mean tare to load	0·96	0·71	1·09	0·71	1·00	0·95
Ratio of mean total moving weight to load	1·94	1·70	2·11	1·72	1·99	1·94
Mean tare per declared B.H.P. Cwts.	2·04	2·37	3·60	4·48	4·80	3·16
Mean total moving weight per declared B.H.P. Cwts.	4·14	5·64	6·98	10·88	9.54	6·48
Declared distribution of weight—	Tons.	Tons.	Tons.	Tons.	Tons.	Tons.
Light, without fuel, water, or attendants—						
Steering	1·498	1·583	1·280	1·437	1·848	1·395
Driving	1·498	1·584	0·958	1·413	1·148	1·571
Running order (without attendants)—						
Steering	2·010	2·160	1·338	1·541	2·054	1·810
Driving	1·802	2·170	1·298	1·717	1·394	1·812
Laden and fully provisioned (including attendants), with load equally distributed over platform—						
Steering	2·396	2·105	1·780	2·915	3·238	2·374
Driving	5·069	6·315	3·218	4·838	3·527	4.908

Manœuvring.

Light—

N.B.—The above manœuvring cannot be taken as comparative merits of the vehicles; the skill of the driver forms the largest factor in smart handling.

Hill-climbing tests.

Light. Loaded—

Time taken to move into position. Minutes	9	6	3½	9	1½	3
Loaded. Time to move out	3½	8	3	Withdrawn	1½	1¾
Weight on driving axle on level. (l) Tons	1·8 / 4·9	1·4 / 3·5	1·7 / 4·8	1·3 / 3·2	2·2 / 6·3	1·8 / 5·1
Total moving weight. (T) Tons	3·7 / 7·3	3·5 / 6·8	3·3 / 7·8	2·7 / 5·0	4·4 / 8·4	3·9 / 7·5
$\frac{D}{T}$	0·49 / 0·67	0·40 / 0·51	0·52 / 0·62	0·48 / 0·64	0·50 / 0·75	0·46 / 0·68
Speed of ascent. Miles per hour—						
1 in 18 macadam (106 yards) from rest	3·50 / 3·87	2·31 / 2·26	3·88 / 2·95	2·91 / 2·49	2·84 / 3·04	2·39 / 2·80
1 in 9½ setts (50 yards)	3·50 / 2·79	— / 1·81	3·07 / 1·88	1·18 / 2·08	2·39 / 4·00	1·35 / 2·98
1 in 13½ macadam (93 yards)	2·93 / 2·95	— / 2·54	1·82 / 1·84	2·68 / 2·19	3·20 / 3·95	2·96 / 3·31
1 in 11 cobbles (87 yards)	2·28 / 3·21	— / 2·22	1·33 / 1·81	2·48 / 2·07	3·17 / 2·69	3·85 / 4·03
Speed of descent. Miles per hour—						
1 in 11 cobbles (87 yards)	2·70 / 2·46	— / 4·45	3·18 / 4·45	2·85 / 3·68	3·74 / 4·08	2·41 / 3·63
1 in 13½ macadam (93 yards)	3·46 / 3·14	— / 4·76	4·23 / 5·29	2·83 / 4·01	5·44 / 4·42	3·30 / 4·89
Speed prior to signal to stop	2·95 / 4·84	— / 4·84	2·66 / 4·12	1·89 / 2·57	5·28 / 12·0	3·50 / 3·55
Distance run before rest. Feet	11·0 / 4·75	94·0	9·0 / 8·0	3·0 / 12·0	90·0	44·5 / 12·5

SECOND LIVERPOOL TRIALS (1899)

SUMMARY OF PARTICULARS OF COMPETING VEHICLES—*continued*

	Thornycroft (No. 1).	Thornycroft (No. 2).	Coulthard (No. 3).	Leyland (No. 5).	Clarkson and Capel (No. 6).	Bayley (No. 9).
Steam Pressure—						
Maximum	185	195	235	200	212	205
Minimum	75	155	190	100	150	75
Average	143	176	213	167	193	174
Total distance covered in trials. Miles	71·5	71·5	35·9	66·8	71·5	71·5
Actual running time	12 h. 2 m.	11 h. 2 m.	6 h. 47 m.	10 h. 50 m.	12 h. 48 m.	12 h. 55 m.
Actual running speed. M.P.H	5·94	6·48	5·29	6·17	5·59	5·54
Commercial duration	13 h. 28 m.	12 h. 37 m.	7 h. 31 m.	13 h. 18 m.	14 h. 29 m.	14 h. 30 m.
Consumption—						
Fuel. Pounds	635 coal.	891 coal	—	—	—	483 coke
Oil. Gallons.	—	—	17¼	35½	71¾	—
Water. Gallons.	511¼	701¼	187¼	267	152¼	332¼
Average load carried. Tons	3·729	6·648	2·322	4·444	3·350	3·668
total moving weight. Tons	7·465	11·602	4·998	7·753	6·765	7·282
,, mean moving weight. Tons	7·235	11·276	4·886	7·636	6·676	7·129
Factors affecting costs per ton-mile—						
Prime cost	£590	£640	£400	£450	£450	£600
Load carried. Tons	3·73	6·65	2·32	4·44	3·35	3·67
Commercial speed. M.P.H.	5·31	5·67	4·78	5·02	4·94	4·93
Ton-miles of load per annum of 260 working days (Table 2)	48,490	86,450	30,160	57,720	43,550	47,710
Fuel consumption—						
Per vehicle mile	8·88 lb. coal	12·46 lb. coal	—	0·539 gal. oil	0·724 gal. oil	6·76 lb. coke
Per ton-mile of load	2·38 lb. coal	1·87 lb. coal	—	0·121 gal. oil	0·216 gal. oil	1·84 lb. coke

Water consumption—						
Per vehicle mile. Gallons	7·15	9·81	—	4·0	2·13	4·65
Per ton-mile of load. Gallons	1·88	1·33	—	0·91	0·64	1·27
Motive power per ton-mile of load	0·27d.	0·22d.	—	0·62d.	1·09d.	0·13d.
Attendants per ton-mile of load (Table 2)	0·44d.	0·36d.	—	0·38d. at 5d. per gal.	0.52d. at 5d. per gal.	0.65d.
Table 1—	35 miles per day, laden.	35 miles per day, laden.		35 miles per day, laden.	35 miles per day, laden.	35 miles per day, laden.
Estimated annual expenditure per annum (260 days). Net	£362. 4s. 7d.	£452. 9s. 8d.	—	£408. 12s. 2d.	£443. 9s. 7d.	£397. 3s. 2d.
Work done ton-miles	33,943	60,515	—	40,404	30,485	33,397
Cost per net ton-mile	2·56d.	1·79d.	—	2·43d.	3·49d.	2·85d.
Table 2—	50 miles per day, laden.	50 miles per day, laden.		50 miles per day, laden.	50 miles per day, laden.	50 miles per day, laden.
Estimated annual expenditure per annum (260 days). Net	£400. 11s. 10d.	£502. 11s. 9d.	—	£480. 3s. 7d.	£529. 14s. 4d.	£431. 16s. 8d.
Work done ton-miles	48,490	86,450	—	57,720	43,550	47,710
Cost per net ton-mile	1·98d.	1·40d.	—	2·00d.	2·92d.	2·17
Table 3—	25 miles, laden, Do. do., light, daily.	25 miles, laden, Do. do., light, daily.		25 miles, laden. Do. do., light, daily.	25 miles, laden, Do. do., light, daily.	25 miles, laden, Do. do., light, daily.
Estimated annual expenditure per annum (260 days). Net	£391. 4s. 6d.	£489. 9s. 6d.	—	£455. 8s. 3d.	£496. 16s. 2d.	£427. 11s. 5d.
Work done ton-miles	24,245	43,225	—	28,860	21,775	23,855
Cost per net ton-mile	3·87d.	2·72d.	—	3·79d.	5·48d.	4·30d.

REMARKS AND CONCLUSIONS ON 1899 LIVERPOOL TRIALS

(1) Thornycroft's system exhibited a most marked advance, it being widely different to 1898; whilst the "Leyland" system, which secured the first award the previous year, was practically the same, with minor improvements.

(2) The vehicles were generally superior to those submitted the previous year, and could be regarded as having arrived at such degree of mechanical excellence and efficiency that their use, in practical operations, would be attended with success and economy compared with horse traction.

(3) Suitable for cart and team owners and others requiring transport of heavy loads. The effective speed was double that of horse-drawn vehicles carrying equal loads; and difficulties of ascending and descending hills were overcome by motor wagons.

(4) The vehicles were capable of competing advantageously for transport of loads from 4 to 6½ tons over distances up to 40 miles, over which a twelve hours' day should suffice for collection, transport, and delivery—assuming Liverpool railway rates.

(5) That 15 per cent on prime cost necessary where work conducted over roads as in trials on such vehicles of the admirable design, workmanship, and material to be found in the two to which gold medals were awarded. The allowance might rise to 30 per cent where the construction had not been so adequately carried out.

(6) Many sources of temporary breakdowns which gave great trouble during 1898 trials were overcome.

(7) Better and more thorough attention should be given to locknuts, collars, splitpins, and effective keying of wheels.

(8) Subject to some improvements in details as in (7) mentioned and to periodic examination and maintenance in thorough working order, the vehicles could be relied upon for regular working—in short, given the recognized principles adopted in all locomotive practice—but the imperfections of common roads were the principal cause of the heavy depreciation and maintenance charges.

(9) *Control and Manœuvring.*—Superior to the best types of

horse-drawn vehicles in general control, and capable of going any-where that horse-drawn vehicles were usually required to go.

(10) *Hill-climbing.*—Greatly superior to horse-drawn vehicles.

(11) *Weight-distribution.*—Serious recommendation to manu-facturers of placing as much weight as possible upon the driving axle. All the vehicles under some conditions would have been more efficient had adhesion been available. The greater propul-sive effort which the engines were in all cases capable of exerting could not be effectually applied in several instances, because the distribution of weight when the wagon was light or when it was laden, and sometimes in both cases, was not sufficiently concen-trated on the driving axles.

(12) *Operating.*—Number of operations generally less than 1898, and there were more satisfactory arrangements of an automatic nature for regulating and controlling the vehicles. All taps, levers, valves, etc., should be in front of or to one side of, and not behind the driver, and should be simplified and disposed for convenient manipulation. Several of the vehicles were so designed and arranged as to admit of an unskilled driver being entrusted with their management.

(13) *Steering.*—Important to have absolute control by means of wheel and worm gearing and to have no play or slackness in the connexions. Direct tillers inadvisable for such traffic; evils might arise from the action of a wheel steering *too* slow. Such gear should be as rapid in action as was consistent with reason-able physical exertion on the driver's part.

(14) *Transmission.*—Both chain and tooth transmission were employed and each had special advantages, and it was undesirable to pronounce in favour of either. Duplicate gear wheels should be carried by all motor vehicles for heavy loads using tooth transmission.

That a two-speed gear or equivalent was essential to success-ful working.

(15) *Fuel.*—Solid fuel was more economical—especially coke, liquid fuel being at a serious disadvantage where costs per net ton-mile were a determining factor. Better means should be employed to intercept particles of dust and soot, which caused a considerable nuisance, especially when boiler was steaming hard.

(16) *Condensers.*—Unless efficiency of a condenser was very

high, where water was procurable at fifteen miles apart it was questionable if a condenser had any advantage. Three of the vehicles using condensers did not lubricate cylinders, which might cause excessive wear; but probably effective filtration or graphite lubrication would meet this objection. The former could not apparently yet be relied on in motor vehicles to prevent lubricants passing into boiler.

(17) *Speed.*—Five miles an hour seemed a suitable limit for very heavy traffic, since at higher speeds deterioration of framework and wheels through vibration and shock rapidly occurred. Should new inventions permit of higher speeds without injury the possibilities of the development of motor traffic for cheap, regular, and fast transport of goods appeared to have no limit.

(18) *Wheels.*—The wheels and tyres were generally efficient, but concentration of heavy loads upon the small area of wheel contact was a serious difficulty, and constituted the chief mechanical cause of the slow progress made in the problem of goods transport by motor vehicles.

Awards: Gold Medals to "Leyland" and "Thornycroft" systems.

THIRD LIVERPOOL TRIALS, 1901

Inherent merits were demonstrated as belonging to self-propelled goods lorries as distinguished from traction engines by the trials of 1898 and 1899, but it was felt that further developments were desirable. Many improvements were made between the first and second trials, when an important advance was made. In order to see whether builders could improve their designs to comply with the then existing tare weight, the third series of trials was held.

There were four classes, as follows :—

Class.	Tons Load.	Max. Tare 2 Tons.	Min. Level Platform Area.	Min. Width Driving Tyres.	Speed.
A	1½ tons	2 tons	45 sq. ft.	3 inches	8 M.P.H.
B	5 ,,	3 ,,	75 ,,	5 ,,	5 ,,
C	5 (minimum)	No limit	95 ,,	6 ,,	5 ,,
D	4 ,,	,,	Not specified	4 ,,	5 ,,

The points taken into consideration in judging were similar to those enumerated in 1899 trials.

Eight competitors entered thirteen vehicles.

Class A.— Geo. F. Milnes & Co., Ltd., 17 Balderton Street, Oxford Street, London, W. (two vehicles).

Class B.—Lancashire Steam Motor Co., Leyland.

Class C.—Thornycroft Steam Wagon Co., Ltd.
C. & A. Musker, Ltd., Tueff Brook, Liverpool— Oil-fired.
Ditto, ditto—Coke-fired.
Simpson & Bibby, Pomona Engine Works, Cornbrook, Manchester.

Class D.—Thornycroft Steam Wagon Co., Ltd. (D 1).
T. Coulthard & Co , Ltd., Cooper Road, Preston.
Mann's Patent Steam Cart and Wagon Co., Ltd., Leeds.
Simpson & Bibby (D 5).

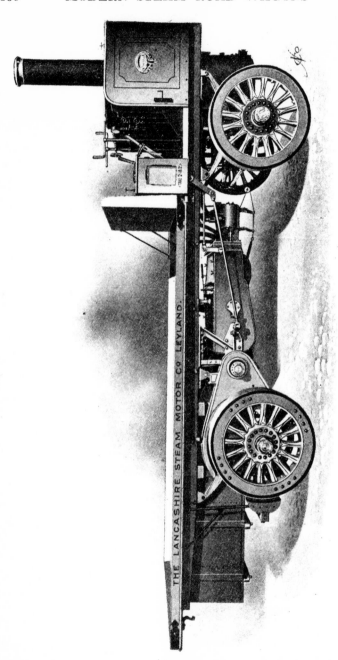

Fig. 77.   The Leyland Lorry, 1905, Liverpool Trials.

VEHICLE No. B 1

THE LANCASHIRE STEAM MOTOR Co., LEYLAND

(Gold medal was awarded this vehicle.)

This vehicle (Fig. 77) was 18 ft. 4 in. long by 6 ft. 5½ in. extreme width. The wheel base 8 ft. 10½ in., and gauge 5 ft. 3¾ in. The platform had 76 ft. available area, and was 3 ft. 7 in. high when light and 3 ft. 4½ in. when loaded with 5 tons. The wheels were of the military type, with steel naves, oak spokes, and ash felloes. The front wheels were 2 ft. 9 in. diameter with 4 in. tyres, and driving wheels 2 ft. 11¼ in. with 5 in. tyres. The chain wheels were attached by bolts through the felloes.

The boiler was of the fire-tube type with 76 sq. ft. of heating surface. Coke fuel was used fed through a central shoot. The grate area was given as 2½ sq. ft. Tough seamless copper tubes were used, and a fusible plug was fixed in the crown plate of the fire box. The boiler was stated to be tested at 450 lb. and the working pressure given as 225 lb., at which the safety valve, blowing into the water tank, was set. An automatic feed pump was worked off the compensating gear shaft, and was so arranged that any excessive water above the amount required for the boiler was pumped back to the tank, the regulation being under hand-wheel control. A small steam pump was used as an auxiliary. The fire was regulated by a hinged ash pan and by the lid covering the central feed shoot. Double check valves were fitted to both pumps, and the safety water gauge was of the " Klinger " pattern.

The engine was horizontal, compound, reversing, with cylinders 3½ in. and 6¼ in. diameter by 6 in. stroke, running at 420 revolutions per minute and developing 25 B.H.P. Good lubrication to all parts was secured by encasing the engine, change gear, compensating and steering gear in dust-proof, oil-tight casings. For emergency both cylinders were capable of being worked with high-pressure steam, the high-pressure cylinder having its own exhaust under these conditions.

The gearing was of steel throughout with machine-cut teeth, the ratio provided 9·8 and 19·6 to 1. A Hans Renolds chain was used for driving. The company's "cushion drive," arranged in the small hollow pinions on the compensating gear shaft, was

M

deemed an important feature as relieving the chains and working parts from initial shocks when starting. The arrangement permits of almost a complete revolution of the engine before the full power—gradually applied—is exerted. To reduce friction a bolt was put through the hollow compensating gear shaft to take the end thrust caused by the bevel wheels off the bearings. By means of an internal clutch operated by a hand lever the compensating gear could be locked. No keys were used in the construction throughout, all wheels being put on flanges. Locked nuts were used throughout.

Two brakes were available: one, of the screw-down type, acting on the hind wheels; the other was a pulley with band on the countershaft.

The water tank was of 138 gal. capacity, and the bunkers 12·2 cubic feet.

VEHICLE No. C 1

THE THORNYCROFT STEAM WAGON Co., Ltd.

(Gold medal was awarded this vehicle.)

This vehicle was 22 ft. 6 in. by 6 ft. 6 in. extreme width; wheel base, 12 ft. 6 in.; wheel gauge, 5 ft. 7 in.; diameter of front wheels, 2 ft. 9 in. with 6 in. tyres; driving wheels, 3 ft. 6 in. diameter with 8 in. tyres. The front axle was mounted on a pivot in the centre, ensuring a three-point support and relieving the frame of transverse twisting actions. The platform was of 95 sq. ft.; 4 ft. 3 in. in height when light, and 4 ft. when loaded with 6½ tons.

The boiler was of the company's patent central-fired steamwagon type, with straight water tubes circularly arranged around the fire. The total heating surface was given as 132 sq. ft., and 4¼ sq. ft. grate area; working pressure 225 lb. per sq. in. Coal or coke fuel could be used, and regulation was obtained by a hinged door in the ash pan and by the shoot cover. Two safety valves were employed—one lifting if the normal pressure was exceeded, and the second was set about 10 lb. above normal pressure and acting in the event of the first failing to act. The

" Reflex " pattern of water gauge was used. The boiler was fed
by a pump driven directly from engine when the wagon was
running; when stationary the engine could be disconnected from
the transmission gear and run free, thus still feeding the boiler;
or the feed water might be supplied by an injector of special
design mounted on the boiler. The cones of this injector can be
removed for examination, adjustment, or cleaning whilst the
boiler is under steam. To effect economy the exhaust steam was
utilized to primarily heat the feed water; and to facilitate
attention a special "clinkering hole" was provided for fire cleaning. The top cover is removable and the tubes cleaned by
passing a steel-wire brush through each. The boiler casing was
easily taken off to allow of readily cleaning soot from the outside
of the tubes.

The engine is horizontal, compound, reversing, having cylinders 4 in. and 7 in. by 5 in. stroke, with a constant lead radial
valve gear of special design permitting of any degree of linking
up. The two cut-off notches were at $\frac{5}{8}$ and $\frac{7}{8}$ of the stroke. The
whole was enclosed in a dust-proof, oil-tight casing; thus the
"splash" method of lubrication was used. The engine was
stated as developing 30 H.P. at 500 revolutions per minute. The
exhaust steam, after passing through the feed-water heater, was
discharged through the smoke box. A spark arrester was fitted
in the smoke box, through which all the flue gases were drawn
by the draught created by the exhaust.

The transmission was the company's patent chainless type,
and fitted with special gear for hill-climbing. A steel machine-
cut pinion on engine crank shaft meshed with a machine-cut
bronze spur wheel on the first portion of the countershaft, which
was in three separate parts, the middle portion being connected
with the first and third by special enclosed large surface universal
couplings, whereby the vertical motion of the bearing springs is
taken up in a mechanical manner, the driving effort on the rear
wheels being continuous even over the roughest roads and under
all conditions of loading. The perch frame found in the company's
1899 patterns is now absent, being replaced by a pair of triangular-
formed brackets, being one form of their patent bell-crank drive,
borne on the rear axle and carrying the third countershaft part
with double-helical cast-steel pinion in a pair of ordinary adjust-

able bearings. The bell crank was prevented from turning round the rear axle by a radius rod hinged to the vehicle under-frame in such manner as to permit full play to the rear bearing springs. The said pinion meshes with a cast-steel spur ring borne on the differential gear, which was carried by the rotating rear axle. The rear axle was itself borne in axle boxes of the locomotive type attached to the centre of the plate rear bearing springs, and the road wheels are finally driven by the Company's patent spring drive, short helical springs in compression being employed in this arrangement. The normal gear ratio was 12·4; the low gear 21·7. The compensating gear was locked by binding the sleeve to a drum on the near side driving wheel by means of a band.

A screw-down brake applying wooden blocks to the rear wheels, reversal of the engine, and a foot-operated band brake were provided for braking purposes.

The bunkers were of 38·2 cub. ft. capacity; the water tank 236½ gal. Apparatus was provided for blowing deposited soot from the outside of the tubes by means of a steam hose. A steam blast was also obtainable for accelerating steam production, and a bye-pass valve was fitted for admitting full boiler pressure to the low-pressure cylinder should increased power be necessary.

VEHICLE No. D 1

THORNYCROFT STEAM WAGON Co., Ltd.

This vehicle was 18 ft. 6 in. long by 6 ft. 5 in. extreme width; wheel base, 10 ft.; wheel gauge, 5 ft. 6½ in.: platform area, 65 sq. ft.; platform height, when light 3 ft. 10 in., when loaded with 4 tons 3 ft. 7½ in.; diameter of front wheels, 2 ft. 9 in., with 4 in. tyres; diameter of hind wheels, 3 ft. 3 in., with 5 in. tyres.

In general design similar to Vehicle No. C 1, but the front axle had no central pivot and a smaller boiler was fitted, of similar pattern as used in 1899. The gear ratios were 10·1 and 17·7. Shoe brakes were fitted, operated by foot lever; reversal of engine constituted secondary brake. The water tanks were of 172 gal. capacity; bunkers, 12·8 cub. ft.

This vehicle was considered of equal merit as No. D 2 (Coulthard), and both were awarded gold medals.

Fig. 78.   Coulthard No. D 2.   1901 Liverpool Trials.

VEHICLE No. D 2

T. COULTHARD & Co., LTD., PRESTON

(Gold medal was awarded this vehicle.)

This vehicle (Fig. 78) was 18 ft. 5½ in. long by 6 ft. 6 in. in width; wheel base, 9 ft. 10½ in.; wheel gauge, 5 ft. 6 in.; platform area, 72½ sq. ft.; height of same, 3 ft. 9 in. light, 3 ft. 6½ in. with 5 tons load; gun-carriage pattern wheels with steel hubs and bronze bushes; diameter of front wheels, 2 ft. 9 in., with 5 in. tyres; driving wheels, 3 ft. diameter, with 6½ in. tyres, fitted with makers' triangular drive, whereby the drive is taken direct to the wheel felloes.

Boiler, etc.—Vertical fire tube with solid drawn-steel tubes electrically galvanized as a protection against corrosion; working pressure, 225 lb.; tested pressure, 450 lb.; grate area, 2¾ sq. ft.; heating surface, 77 sq. ft. The boiler is placed behind the front axle for the following reasons; (1) for increased tractive force, (2) to secure more weight on driving wheels when running light, (3) to relieve the front wheels, and (4) to enable the driver to have an uninterrupted view of the ground in front.

An auxiliary steam pump was fitted, having separate suction from the tank and a separate delivery and check valve on boiler. The two check valves were so constructed that they could be examined whilst under steam. An automatic feed pump, worked off the end of second-motion shaft by eccentric, with enclosed dirt and grit-proof casing for ram, was also fitted. The feed pump and feed-water heater were also self-contained with the casing.

The engine was compound with link reversing gear and piston valves, developing 25 B.H.P. at 450 revolutions per minute, with cylinders 3¾ in. and 7 in. diameter and 6 in. stroke. A distinguishing feature in the engine was the arrangement of the valves and main cover. Only one cover was used for both cylinders and piston valves, which also served as a receiver whilst supporting the multiplier used for admitting live steam to the low-pressure cylinder, the exhaust from the high-pressure being diverted to atmosphere. The "multiplier" served also as a relief valve, any damage through accumulation of water in cylinders being thus avoided. Stuffing boxes were not used.

The steam regulator consisted of a balanced valve attached to the high-pressure cylinder steam chest.

The crank shaft was cut out of a solid steel billet, and carried, with the eccentrics, in two long bearings. On one end was a pinion engaging with a gear wheel on the second-motion shaft. On a square in the middle of this shaft were a pair of unequal pinions, either of which might be made to engage with corresponding gear wheels carried on the crown of the compensating gear. The compensating gear shaft was the only one projecting through the casing. The whole of the gearing, running in a bath of oil, was of cast steel, machine-cut, no keys being used in the transmission gear.

The compensating gear shaft was carried in long bushed bearings attached to the casing, and these bushes were in turn carried in spherical bearings supported in cast-steel brackets rigidly bolted to the frame. The method of supporting the cylinder end allowed of a ball-and-socket motion, so that the engine, motion work, gearing, and shafts, being self-contained in a rigid casing, were kept in accurate mesh and alignment, whilst the method of suspension allowed the main frame some elasticity and spring without setting up internal strains and cross wind in the transmission gear.

The tank was of 180 gal. capacity, and the bunkers 10·8 cub. ft. The brake was of the double-acting band type, consisting of steel cables lined with hard wood blocks coiled round the brake drum. The platform was hinged at the back to permit inspection of engine and gearing.

This vehicle was considered by the judges of equal merit to D 1 (Thornycroft), and both were awarded gold medals.

VEHICLE No. D 3

MANN'S PATENT STEAM CART AND WAGON Co., Ltd., LEEDS

This vehicle's dimensions were as follows: length, 13 ft. 6 in.; width, 6 ft. 6 in.; wheel base, 8 ft. 3 in.; wheel gauge, 4 ft. 3 in.; 34½ sq. ft. available goods-carrying area; height of platform, 4 ft. 3 in. light, 4 ft. ½ in. loaded with 5 tons. The frame could be tipped, and a windlass was provided for hauling it back again.

The steering axle turned about its centre and carried the front wheels, which were 2 ft. 9 in. in diameter. The cart was separately constructed and carried two driving wheels 4 ft. in diameter with 5 in. tyres, connected to and rotated by the engine road wheels, of same diameter and width of tyre. The two together made the width of tyre 10¼ in. on each side of the engine.

The boiler was of the locomotive type with mild steel plates hydraulically riveted ; working pressure, 160 lb. per sq. in. The engine was horizontal and compound, with cylinders 4 in. and 6¾ in. diameter by 8 in. stroke. Reversing was effective by the company's patent reversing gear. The driving axle was a live one 3¼ in. in diameter. Two brakes were fitted : one a band brake acting upon a pulley on the intermediate shaft and one upon the rim of the wheel of the vehicle. The water tanks gave a capacity of 144 gal. and the bunkers 3·4 cub. ft.

VEHICLE No. D 4

MANN'S PATENT STEAM CART AND WAGON Co., Ltd., LEEDS

This vehicle is illustrated in Fig. 79. The dimensions were as follows : length, 18 ft. 11 in. ; width, 6 ft. 5 in. ; wheel base, 11 ft. ½ in. ; wheel gauge, 4 ft. 3 in. ; carrying area, 69·8 sq. ft. ; height, 4 ft. 2 in. light and 4 ft. when carrying 5 tons ; driving wheels, 3 ft. 6 in. diameter, with 5 in. tyres = 10¼ in. on each side of engine.

In general construction this was the same as No. D 3, except that the engine was carried on a rear extension of the fire-box side plates instead of on the boiler. The water-tank capacity 158 gal. and the bunkers 5·8 cub. ft.

Silver medal was awarded the makers in the trials.

Two other makers, Messrs. C. & A. Musker, Ltd., Liverpool, and Messrs. Simpson & Bibby, also competed, but as neither of these makers' types completed the trials or have since been commercially used, there would be nothing gained in describing or including them in the results.

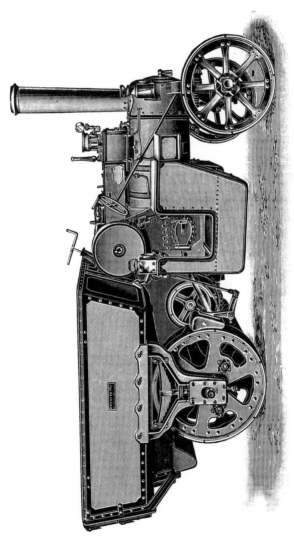

Fig. 79.   Mann No. D 4.   1901 Liverpool Trials.

LAST LIVERPOOL TRIALS, 1901

SUMMARY OF PARTICULARS OF COMPETING VEHICLES

	B 1 LEYLAND.	C 1 THORNYCROFT.	D 1 THORNYCROFT.	D 2 COULTHARD.	D 3 MANN.	D 4 MANN.
Dimensions over all	18' 4" × 6' 5½" / 8' 7"	22' 6" × 6' 6" / 9' 4"	18' 6" × 6' 5" / 8' 10"	18' 5½" × 6' 6" / 8' 9½"	13' 6" × 6' 6" / 8' 0"	18' 11" × 6' 5" / 8' 3"
Dimensions of level platform	12' 5" × 6' 1½"	14' 10" × 6' 5"	11' 7¾" × 5' 7"	12' 1" × 6' 0"	5' 8" × 6' 1"	11' 8½" × 5' 11½"
Ratio of available platform area to extreme moving area in any horizontal plane	0·64	0·65	0·55	0·60	0·39	0·58
Diameter of wheels in inches	33 and 35¼	33 and 42	33 and 39	33 and 36	33 and 48	33 and 42
Width of tyres in inches	4 and 5	6 and 8	4 and 5	5 and 6½	5 and 10¼	5 and 10¼
Height of platform, loaded. In inches	40½	48	43·5	42·5	48·5	48
Mean deflection of springs under load. In inches	2·5	3	2·5	2·5	2·5	2
Angle of lock. Degrees	33	42	38·5	37	36·5	5
Boiler—						
Heating surface. Square feet.	76	132	83	77	51	51
Capacity to mean glass. Gallons	25	38	22	19	31	31
Declared working pressure	225	225	200	225	160	29·5
Grate area. Square feet	2·5	4·25	2·4	2·75	2·5	2·5
Engine—						
Cylinders. Stroke	3·5 and 6·25 / 6	4 and 7 / 5	4 and 7 / 5	3·75 and 7 / 6	4 and 6·4 / 8	4 and 6·4 / 8
Revolutions per minute	420	500	440	450	360	360
Declared B.H.P.	25	25	20	25	25	25
Ratio of gearing between engine shaft and driving wheels	9·8 and 19·6	12·4 and 21·7	10·1 and 17·7	8·8 and 17·2	13 and 32	9 and 20
Capacity—						
Fuel. Cubic feet	12·2	38·2	12·8	10·8	3·4	5·8
Water. Gallons	138	236	172	180	144	158
Load carried. Tons	4·813	6·331	4·423	4·481	3·612	4·460
Tare—						
Without fuel, water, or stores. Tons	2·975	6·400	3·800	3·700	3·999	3·989
Fully provisioned, not including attendants	4·023	8·120	5·044	5·067	5·137	5·222
Mean (not including attendants)	3·742	7·650	4·700	4·656	4·776	4·821

Total moving weight—						
Laden and fully provisioned (including attendants)	8·910	14·504	9·527	9·626	8·828	9·757
Mean. In tons	8·629	14·034	9·183	9·215	8·467	9·356
Ratio of mean tare to load	0·78	1·21	1·06	1·04	1·32	1·08
Ratio of mean total moving weight to load	1·79	2·22	2·08	2·05	2·34	2·09
Mean tare per declared B.H.P. at stated revolutions of engine. Cwts.	2·99	6·12	4·70	3·62	3·82	3·86
Mean total moving weight per declared B.H.P. at stated revolutions of engine. Cwts.	6·90	11·23	9·18	7·37	6·77	7·49
Manœuvring—						
Time taken to move into position. Min. Sec.	2 57	4 7	1 0	4 5	1 1	0 34
Time taken to return to shed	0 39	0 46	0 42	0 30	0 57	1 2
Hill-climbing tests— (1) Light, (2) Loaded.						
Weight on driving axle on level. (D) Tons	{ 2·25, 4·76 }	{ 5·38, 6·77 }	{ 2·90, 3·75 }	{ 2·95, 4·91 }	{ 3·19, 4·75 }	{ 3·02, 4·86 }
Total moving weight. (T) Tons	{ 3·77, 8·41 }	{ 7·65, 14·02 }	{ 4·63, 8·75 }	{ 4·60, 9·46 }	{ 4·75, 9·25 }	{ 4·70, 9·78 }
$\dfrac{D}{T}$	0·60	0·70	0·63	0·64	0·67	0·64
Speed of ascent. Miles per hour—						
1 in 18 macadam from rest (106 yards)	{ 3·14, 3·01 }	{ 3·52, 3·13 }	{ 3·28, 2·97 }	{ 3·62, 2·82 }	{ 3·89, 2·91 }	{ 3·29, 2·29 }
1 in 9½ setts (50 yards)	{ 2·64, 2·55 }	{ 3·99, 2·56 }	{ 3·47, 2·37 }	{ 3·78, 2·73 }	{ 3·17, 2·70 }	{ 3·96, 2·36 }
1 in 13½ macadam (90 yards)	{ 4·01, 2·95 }	{ 4·92, 3·22 }	{ 4·25, 3·46 }	{ 3·60, 3·54 }	{ 5·35, 3·38 }	{ 4·12, 3·37 }
1 in 11 cobbles (87 yards)	{ 3·17, 2·99 }	{ 2·81, 2·56 }	{ 3·90, 3·13 }	{ —, 3·14 }	{ 3·68, 2·71 }	{ 3·40, 3·25 }
Speed of descent. M.P.H.—						
1 in 11 cobbles	{ 3·97, 3·26 }	{ 2·72, 4·03 }	{ 3·26, 3·96 }	{ 2·97, 3·01 }	{ 3·81, 3·54 }	{ 3·82, 4·51 }
1 in 13½ macadam	{ 4·44, 4·13 }	{ 3·72, 3·43 }	{ 4·80, 4·65 }	{ 2·65, 4·10 }	{ 3·58, 3·50 }	{ 3·44, 4·72 }

LAST LIVERPOOL TRIALS, 1901

SUMMARY OF PARTICULARS OF COMPETING VEHICLES—*continued*

	B 1 LEYLAND.	C 1 THORNYCROFT.	D 1 THORNYCROFT.	D 2 COULTHARD.	D 3 MANN.	D 4 MANN.
Control on declivity of 1 in 9 (setts)—						
Speed during rev. prior to signal	5·34 / 3·36	3·51 / 3·13	4·21 / 3·39	3·58 / 4·22	2·75 / 2·66	5·17 / 5·46
Distance run before coming to rest. Feet	19·4 / 15·5	8·6 / 13·6	14·9 / 8·3	6·5 / 15·4	11·2 / 14·9	15·5 / 13·7
Total distance covered in trials. Miles	167·3	166·8	166·6	148·7	166·6	166·6
Time occupied. Min. Sec.	28 21	27 34	26 44	26 10	31 47	23 24
Steam pressure—						
Maximum	240	240	195	220	190	210
Minimum	160	175	150	60	85	100
Average	212	209	175	150	147	165
Stoppages to adjust	None	None	4	None	1	1
Consumption. Fuel. Pounds—						
Gas coke	·	3232	2439	2518	2480	2839
Water. Gallons	2030	1935	1397	1527	1533	1653
	1098				tank leaking slightly	continuous slight leakage
Average running speed. M.P.H.	6·04	6·05	6·23	5·68	5·24	7·12
Average load carried. Tons	4·813	6·331	4·423	4·481	3·612	4·469
Average total moving weights. Tons	8·910	14·504	9·527	9·626	8·828	9·757
Average mean moving weights. Tons	8·629	14·034	9·183	9·215	8·467	9·356
Factors affecting the costs per net ton-mile—						
Prime cost	£530	£750	£650	£535	£465	£500
Gross ton-miles during trials	1443·6	2340·2	1529·9	1370·3	1410·6	1558·7
Ton-miles of load during trials	805·2	1056·0	736·9	666·3	601·8	744·5
Commercial speed. M.P.H.	6·04	6·01	6·23	5·85	5·23	7·11
Fuel consumption per gross ton-mile. Pounds	1·41	1·38	1·59	1·84	1·76	1·82
Do. per ton-mile of load. Pounds	2·52	3·06	3·31	3·78	4·12	3·81
Water consumption—						
Per gross ton-mile. Gallons	0·77	0·83	0·91	1·12	1·09	1·06
Per ton-mile of load	1·36	1·83	1·90	2·29	2·52	2·22
Motive power per ton-mile. Pence	0·219	0·268	0·289	0·331	0·361	0·333

INDEX